THE NEW ADVENTURES
OF FRANKENSTEIN 1

Frankenstein Lives Again

Frankenstein Lives Again

by
Donald F. Glut

MEWS BOOKS
LONDON AND CONNECTICUT

A Mews Original Publication
© Mews Books Limited 1977

*

FIRST MEWS PAPERBACK EDITION JANUARY 1977

*

Mews Books are published by
Mews Books Limited, 20 Bluewater Hill, Westport, Connecticut 06880
and distributed by
New English Library Limited, Barnard's Inn, Holborn, London EC1N 2JR.
Made and printed in Great Britain by Hunt Barnard Printing Ltd., Aylesbury, Bucks.

45200060 2

CHAPTER 1

Frozen Horror

Fairfax looked hysterically at the fuel gauge of the instrument panel. The airplane seemed to belch as it tossed in the powerful wind. Again he checked the instruments, hoping that they would miraculously spring back to life. To his consternation, they remained locked, frozen as were the barren wastes that flashed past the cockpit.

'Empty!' he shouted, his voice hardly carrying over the whining of the craft as it plunged earthward. 'Not a drop of fuel! What a fool I was to come this far!'

His strong hands clutched the cold stick, trying vainly to yank the ship out of its death trajectory. The plane choked for fuel that was not there, it seemed to gasp as Fairfax was gasping. Massive stretches of ice sped by the cockpit windshield as the nose of the craft dipped closer to the bleak earth.

Fairfax knew that he was about to crash, that there was nothing that could avert his fate. He was going to die; he knew that, but refused to meet death without exhausting himself first in the struggle to survive. Had he known how to pray, he would have, but instead he maintained his insane grip on the guide stick.

More peaks of ice flew past his vision until all he could see was a blur of whiteness and frozen gauges. The droning of the airplane drowned his ears. The earth shot up faster. A terrible wall of ice and snow seemed to appear before him and the craft was suddenly attempting to break through the irresistible barrier. Absorbed by the mountain of packed snow, the plane arced, its tail section wavering for a few moments in the wind, then died. Fairfax hurt for only a moment.

A small group of eskimos huddled together as they saw the gleaming ship vanish amid the swirling snow.

'It is an airplane,' Norcha assured the others. 'It has fallen near the sacred tomb of the Ice God!'

Norcha's face, worn hard and brown by a long life in the severe cold, looked sternly at his companions. They had all seen the ship plunge toward the ground, but it was only Norcha who had stood beyond the white hill and actually pinpointed the craft's earthbound location.

'You are certain?' one of the eskimos inquired, fearfully. 'Remember, Norcha, the sacred tomb. Perhaps this is an omen, a messenger that we have not been faithful to the Ice God.'

'You talk nonsense, Bruk,' said Norcha. 'Airplanes come from men and not gods. Inside was a man, like us. But, even though unintentionally, he has invaded our holy grounds and profaned the land of the Ice God.'

A third member of the group said, 'But Norcha, this is a sacrilege on the part of the stranger. Sacrilege! If the Ice God would awaken, his vengeance would be upon us and our children.'

'You are right,' Norcha replied grimly, stroking his lined jaw. He clenched his gloved fist and the shaggy hood of his parka moved with the wrinkling of his brow. 'The outsider must be kept away from the sacred tomb!'

With parkas contrasting against the miles and miles of undiminishing whiteness, the band of eskimos looked to their leader for advice.

'Show us where the stranger is, Norcha,' said Bruk.

For a few moments, Norcha paused in thought, his nostrils fighting the cold wind that whirled into his face. 'He can walk to the sacred tomb within minutes. That is how near he is to the holy place. We must hurry if we are to reach the tomb before he does.'

There was no further delaying. Norcha's expressionless eyes scanned the area around him and his companions, stopping at the sleds and teams of huskies, which barked from boredom.

'We shall be there shortly with the dogsleds,' said Norcha, leading the others to their only method of transportation across the white reaches of the North. Within seconds, the eskimos had boarded the sleds and were commanding the canines. The animals barked as if competing with the howling wind. They were on their way to meet the stranger who dared to profane the sacred tomb of the Ice God.

Miraculously, Fairfax was reviving. His brain told him that he was a corpse. And yet he could move. Somehow, he had been saved by the wall of snow into which the craft had plunged.

Whiteness packed solid against the windshield of the plane and the cockpit must have been as cold as the winds outside. For several minutes, Fairfax hardly moved, preferring to marvel at still being alive. He shivered from the subzero temperature and tried to keep moving in order to booster his circulation. At last he rubbed his hands together, producing hardly enough heat to keep him warm. He wished he were wearing gloves. He should have been dead and as he began to move in the pilot's seat he started thinking that he had been saved for some unfathomable purpose.

Unfastening the seat belt, Fairfax struggled to stand. Mechanically, his hands began to ignore the cold and search for something. He knew where he had left it, a small metal box behind the pilot's seat.

'Here it is,' he said to himself. 'Still there . . . and still intact, I hope.'

Patting himself a few times to stimulate his blood, Fairfax stooped down to pick up the metal box. He placed it on the seat, flicked the latches, and opened it.

'Good,' he thought, 'the cotton layers kept it from breaking.'

Fairfax smiled, the first time since he had learned that his fuel was going, when he removed the flask of whiskey from the box. Quickly, he removed the cap and began to guzzle down the golden liquid. Almost immediately the warmth began to surge through his veins.

'That's good. Makes me warm.'

Caring less than before about the cold, Fairfax put on his gloves and made his way through the cockpit to the exit of the plane. He opened it and, taking in a deep breath of the chilling air, stepped outside with newly found courage. His face was attacked by the stinging wind but the protective alcohol within him helped ward off the otherwise, torturous elements. The

North seemed to howl at him, jeer him for being a fool, while the scenery was no more than monotonous piles of whiteness of varying shapes and sizes.

He quaffed more of the liquid and felt better.

As Fairfax's vision began to get hazy from the whiskey taking command over his body, he heard a distant sound that might prove to be his salvation. He strained to hear the yelping and barking of dogs, which were gradually getting louder and, he hoped, closer. For dogs could mean sleds and sleds might mean a rescue party. Perhaps someone watched him crash, he thought hopefully, and would save him from the biting cold.

He was hardly worrying anymore about getting back to civilization. Now he was happy, if not from the thoughts of rescue then for the whiskey. He began to laugh.

Moving with no real destination, he began to proceed, stumbling through the snow to keep his blood circulating. He had no desire to have his rescue party discover a human icicle. Perhaps he would even intercept them.

Briefly, Fairfax turned to look back at the plane. The nose was completely buried in the mountain of snow. The posterior section of the ship stuck out of the embankment like a dart. They would never dig that out, he thought, then proceeded on his hike.

Fairfax paid hardly any attention to where he walked. The chunks of ice, and the effect of the whiskey, made him occasionally stumble. Several times he lost his balance and fell forward into the cushioning snow. But the whiskey always made him forget the cold and drove him onward.

The barking of the dogs was louder, increasing his belief that he was about to be rescued. Consuming the last few drops of alcohol, Fairfax tossed the bottle into the whistling wind, confident that one of the approaching animals would be a friendly Saint Bernard with a keg of brandy around its neck.

Fairfax staggered, swayed. His feet were beginning to fail him more than ever. His stumbling and falling were more frequent than before. But he went on to the music of howling wind and dogs. The realization came to him that he could not go much farther or even remain conscious for any great length of time. His feet were losing all their feeling. The only hope he had was in the dogs. But if they did not find him his life was worthless.

With one final surge of energy, Fairfax tried to heave himself forward. The veins in his neck bulged as he attempted going on but failed dismally. His gloved fingers ripped into the snow and tried to make a handhold with the small pieces of ice. Straining, he managed to drag himself forward – slowly, agonizingly – until he struck *something.*

He mumbled incoherently, then raised his eyes, peering through the frost covered lids. Fairfax raised one shaking hand before his face. The gusts of wintry air were almost impossible to breathe. Fingers, nearly totally numb, barely felt the touch of the smooth surface before him.

'It's hard . . . ' he thought. 'Like a block of ice.'

The other hand gripped snow. He yanked himself closer to whatever it was that was before him. His freezing body managed to inch its way a bit nearer. Fairfax's head lay flush against the wall of glassy ice that blocked his way. Somehow he managed to muster the strength to raise himself up against the block of ice that stood like a frozen wall.

'Wh-what?' he gasped, his eyes staring incredulously at the object that towered some eight feet into the air.

The dogs were exceedingly close now. And through the noises of their barking, Fairfax thought he heard human voices babbling in some unknown tongue. But Fairfax did not care about the sounds. His attention was entirely focused upon the wall of ice and the dark form that lay within.

His mind grew steadily duller. Nevertheless he continued to gape into the glasslike obstacle, constantly refocusing his eyes, at the unknown *thing* inside which rested motionless as if in an icy tomb.

Aching but not caring, Fairfax had to know what was within the ice. He had already forgotten the pain of the cold. Stiffly he brushed away the loose snow that had settled upon the glassy wall. Peering through the ice, Fairfax managed to perceive two long human legs. There was a man trapped within the ice, he thought. But judging from the length of those legs, he must surely be a giant.

Fairfax's bulging eyes rose higher, passing the long, yellowish fingers that hung motionless from the lanky yet obviously muscular arms. The size might have been an optical trick of the ice, working like a magnifying glass he rationalized. But he wanted to get a better look at the awesome form that rose like a god in the ice. He saw that one of the massive fists was raised as if attempting to make a final effort to smash its way out of its prison. As he slid himself up the surface of the ice block, he stared up at the head of the creature, which was too high for him to see whether intoxicated or not.

Louder were the barkings and sounds of human voices.

Trembling, Fairfax pulled himself so that he was finally standing upright. Now he stood tall against the block of ice. His feet were almost even with those of the entombed giant. Fairfax himself stood over six feet tall, and yet this creature stood more than two feet talled than he. The pilot pressed his face harder against the sheet of ice, attempting to look up into the face of the being.

'By God, it can't be!' he exclaimed, coughing, gawking at the pale yellow countenance that was a hideous mockery of a man. He could see the ghastly scars, the coarsely sewn wounds. Fairfax, who had been thoroughly intrigued by the emprisoned giant, was now completely revolted by its sheer ugliness. Although overcome by nausea, he could not take his eyes away from the creature, whose face seemed to hold him like a hypnotic vise. The cruel mouth on the creature seemed to be petrified into a perpetual, hate-filled scowl, directed toward Fairfax.

The dogs were almost upon him, barking anxiously. Human voices filled his ears with meaningless jibberish.

Still staring into the face of the monstrous form in the ice, Fairfax moaned, then slumped mercifully into the oblivion of the snow.

CHAPTER 2

Sometimes Legends Are Based on Fact

'He was soon borne away by the waves and lost in the darkness and distance. Thus ends the thrilling saga of Frankenstein and the Monster he created. The end.'

The stocky French gentleman sucked on his empty pipe almost in rhythm with the clacking monotone of the train wheels, then closed the paperback book. For a few moments he started at the bold red logo on the cover.

'*Frankenstein*, by Mary W. Shelley.'

'That was a good novel,' he said with his French accent to the man seated next to him on the passenger car. 'Thank you for letting me read it. It certainly helped pass the hours.'

A smile curled his upper lip which was lined by a small mustache. The black hairs pointed toward his rosy cheeks.

'But here, you may have it back now.'

'Thank you,' said the man next to him. He accepted the book and held onto it covetously.

The man who now held the book was in the vicinity of thirty years old, considerably younger than the other man. His features were ruggedly handsome, with wavy brown hair and a look of high intelligence about him.

Smiling courteously, he said, 'I'm glad you liked the book, my friend. These long train rides can get boring. I'd have taken a plane myself, but planes don't land in this vicinity. I was extremely lucky to find a train that would take me as far as this one goes.'

The younger man glanced out the window. The shade was

13

pulled halfway down to shield his eyes from the blinding sun. Although they were chugging through small towns, desolate wastes of whiteness painted the scenery as far as he could see.

'The far North certainly is barren, isn't it?' he said.

'I know,' replied the man with the mustache. 'Don't the people out there ever come out of their homes? It seems we've been traveling for hours and only have seen a few animals running about.' Again he sipped on his cold pipe, making slurping noises. 'Say, what are you doing out this way, if you don't mind my clumsy attempt at conversation.'

'Not at all,' the younger man said, turning and smiling. 'I'm out here because of this.' He raised the paperback novel as if putting it on exhibition. 'The book you just read.'

'*Frankenstein?*' His eyebrows moved up and down. 'An old gothic horror novel brings you up to this cold hell? I'm afraid you'll have to really give me an explanation, now, monsieur. I am now totally confused,' he laughed.

The youthful passenger frowned for a moment, then responded with a warm smile. 'Yes, *Frankenstein, or The Modern Prometheus*, written by a teenaged girl, Mary Wollstonecraft Shelley. It was first published in 1818. That book is what brought me on this journey to the Arctic.'

The Frenchman cleared his throat and rubbed his sun-tanned chin. He looked intently at the book which the other man held with the reverance usually given to a Bible.

He waited, trying to reason the situation in his mind, then inquired, 'Pardon me if I again seem too concerned with your affairs, or nosey, as you Americans put it, but you are telling me that a book written some hundred and fifty years ago got you on this old railroad train? On a journey to the wilderness of the Arctic? Now you've really got me hanging by a thread, monsieur. You must simply tell me everything. Otherwise I fear I'll never have another night of sleep in my life.'

'All right,' said the American, grinning and extending his hand for a firm shake. 'All right, then, I'll tell you. We've got a ways to go and I don't mind talking. You undoubtedly won't believe a word of what I am about to tell you, but here goes anyway. First off, my name is Winslow. Dr Burt Winslow.'

'Good to know you, Dr Winslow,' said the Frenchman, raising his eyebrows as he pronounced the American's title.

'Burt, please.'

14

'All right, Burt, if you prefer,' he returned. 'And I am Dupré. Pierre Dupré. I work for a lumber company in Alaska. Sort of on a vacation right now. I am going to visit some friends up at a communications outpost at the Pole. Hmmmff! Some vacation.'

For the first time in a long while, Dupré lowered the pipe and placed it into his lap.

'But tell me, Burt,' he went on, 'just what type of doctor are you? A general practitioner? Specialist?'

'No, nothing like that, Pierre,' said Winslow. 'I'm a scientist. And when you hear my story, you'll probably think I'm a mad scientist. I am a specialist, however. Specialize in biology and electro-chemistry.'

Dupré nodded. 'Hmmm. That sounds like a reason for your interest in *Frankenstein*,' he said laughingly, hardly believing his own words. He expected Winslow to correct him.

'Precisely. That's one of the reasons I'm so fascinated by the account of Frankenstein.'

'Account?' Dupré's eyes popped. 'Just a minute, Burt. You mean *novel* don't you? Not account. I mean, a scientist couldn't possibly believe that Mary Shelley's story was – er, was . . .'

'Fact?' Winslow interjected with an impish look on his face, his eyes sparkling with anticipation of being asked to go on with his explanation.

'Yes.'

'Certainly. I believe it to be fact.'

'But,' Dupré continued, his eyes even wider.

'Now don't get ahead of me, Pierre. I'll explain everything as I go along.'

Winslow took out a cigarette and lit it, inhaling several long drags before he continued speaking. The smoke that issued from his mouth seemed to take on awesome, demonic shapes which became alive with his every word, then dissipated, as he told an incredible tale to the man seated next to him.

CHAPTER 3

Castle Frankenstein

'To begin, my friend, I have always been a man of financial means. You might go so far to say that I was a spoiled play-boy, supported entirely by my parents. My father put me through the best universities in the world. I repaid him by always being the top student in my class and the foremost athelete in all the sports in which I chose to participate. When my father died, I was still away at school. Being the only child, I inherited the entire family fortune.

'Enough of too much past history, Pierre. It is my interest in Frankenstein and his monster that you want to know.

'Ever since I can remember, even as a small boy, I was terribly bored by the mundane. It was always I that organized my playmates in creative play. It was always I who was known as the weird one of the group, the one who did things differently than most other children. I became involved in various hobbies. But most of my free time became occupied by an interest in science. For a while, like Victor Frankenstein himself, the scientist who created what the world now knows as the monster, I became enthralled by the secrets of life and death.

'No, I never desired to go, as Frankenstein had done, into graveyards and charnel houses and even slaughter houses for dead organs, to piece them together into a patchwork mockery of a human being and then endow that creature with life. But although I never wanted to create life in this fashion myself, I did become obsessed with the idea that one man might have accomplished that feat almost two hundred years ago.

'I read *Frankenstein* and re-read it, over and over again. The more I dwelt upon Mary Shelley's words the more I began to believe that they were not mere fiction, but true. Perhaps Victor Frankenstein, unburdened as we are today by so many established rules of science, did create a man, or monster if you prefer, and perhaps he did, as Mary's husband Percy Shelley had always dreamed, give it the gift of eternal life.

'The thought became an obsession with me. The only way to get this Frankenstein business out of my system was to learn whether or not the story was true. All the money I would ever need to sponsor my quest for the truth was at my disposal. And so I decided to take a plane to the very town in which Victor Frankenstein created his being, to Ingoldstadt in Germany.

'If the monster were surely created in Ingoldstadt, there would undoubtedly be some record of the event in that town. The creature, according to the book, was so hideous that even Frankenstein ran from it. Today you can see the effect the monster has had on his maker. For many people confuse the name of the monster with his creator, calling him simply "Frankenstein".

'Ingoldstadt was a small town, yet it was larger than I had expected, it is typically Germanic, something which I might have suspected to find in a picture illustrating the Bavaria of another century. Many of its residents wore the short, leather pants I had expected them to wear, and frequented the local inns where there seemed no more enjoyable passtime than joining in with their friends in an ornate stein of beer.

'The residents were friendly enough to me. I could speak German fluently even before I took it as a subject in school, and so could converse with any of them like a native. However, I detected an air of superstition about most of the townspeople and thought it best, for the present, not to go inquiring among them about monsters. I received directions to reach the office of the Mayor of Ingoldstadt and hastened to make an appointment to see him, all the while being careful not to make any previous mention of the name "Frankenstein".

'Mayor Krag was a roly poly type of character, with the rosiest cheeks I had ever seen, and a long white mustache that he liked to twirl. There was a sparkle in his eyes that made me think of Santa Clause. He greeted me with a strong handshake and smiled.

' "Yes, Herr Winslow," said Mayor Krag. "You have traveled a long way just to come to our little town and see me. Your business must be extremely important."

' "Yes, incredibly important – to me."

' "Then tell me and perhaps I'll be able to help you."

' "All right," I said, anticipating a change in attitude on Krag's part as soon as I told him why I had come to Europe. I studied his face as I spoke so that I could watch the alteration of his features. "I have come about a matter that took place in this town almost two hundred years ago."

'He seemed to know what I was going to say, for the sparkle that had been in his eyes suddenly became extinguished.

' "Yes?" he said in a drawn-out word, raising one eyebrow suspiciously. "And what might that be?"

'I stated slowly, "Frankenstein."

'Krag's eyes bulged. He made a fist with his right hand and slammed it hard upon his paper littered desk.

' "Frankenstein!" he exclaimed, his face twisting into a frown. *"Nein!"*

' "But . . . " I started.

'He cut me off. "Frankenstein is a name we do not speak in Ingoldstadt. It suggests only the worst possible horrors. Horrors which we have been trying to forget."

' "But, *mein herr*, you do not understand."

' "Understand? Harrumphf! What is there not to understand? You are prying into our past, a past which we have endeavored to keep secret for almost two centuries. I suggest you go back to the United States, Dr Winslow."

'There was no chance in me leaving Ingoldstadt until I had found what I wanted and proven that the creation of Frankenstein was fact, and not just the superstitious fantasy of those townspeople.

' "Then if you will not help me," I said sternly, "then I'll search this town for someone who will."

'Krag obviously held back his anger. "You mean you would start asking questions? That I cannot have. It is best that the people do not know why you are here. Although it is against my principles, I'll tell you what you want to know. But I am trusting you as a doctor to be scrupulous with your information."

'The Mayor sat down in his comfortably cushioned chair and

18

folded his hands. I leaned forward on the desk, not wanting to miss a single word.

'At first, he told me what I, and any reader of the novel *Frankenstein*, had already known.

' "The legend has it that almost two hundred years ago, a young scientist from Switzerland, named Victor Frankenstein, while attending the University of Ingoldstadt, became obsessed with the idea that he could create a living man. There are stories that Frankenstein took parts of different corpses and pieced them together to make his hideous monster. Then he brought this horror to life. The monster did not remain in Ingoldstadt long, but for the short time it did, it created only misery, terror, and death."

'I tried to keep back my enthusiasm and delight, but Mayor Krag was telling me the words I had wanted to hear ever since I first considered the truth of *Frankenstein*.

' "And where did he do this?" I inquired. Mrs Shelley's novel was very vague about the creation of the monster. Apparently, Frankenstein had set up a small laboratory in a very unspectacular apartment. But her account was not entirely accurate, as I shall later explain.

' "Frankenstein," he said, "or so the legend says, had come from a well-to-do family. He used his money to purchase an old castle, which has existed since medieval times, on a hilltop just outside of the town. It has come to be known as Castle Frankenstein.

' "Some men say that the Devil himself worked with Frankenstein in that lonely fortress. The castle served as his laboratory of evil and also as a home while he was away from his real home in Geneva. The stories have it that one night the castle became alive with strange lights and noises. That was when the monster without a soul first walked, an event for which our ancestors and we, their descendants, have been eternally sorry."

'Quickly, I asked, "But this Castle Frankenstein where you say the monster was created. What of it? You implied that it still exists."

' "Yes, the castle remains on its ominous place on the hill. The castle overlooks the river. No one goes near it unless they have to. For there are still legends about the place. Some say that the ghost of Frankenstein's Monster still haunts that evil place."

19

' "And who is the present owner of the castle?" I asked.

' "Castle Frankenstein belongs to Ingoldstadt," he explained. "It did before Frankenstein purchased it, and when he abandoned it, the castle went back to our government. But even we have nothing to do with it. The police, when they took possession of the castle, refused to go inside, lest some other blasphemous creation of Frankenstein be lurking through those darkened catacombs. No one has ever wanted that castle since those dark days of Victor Frankenstein."

'A thought was lingering in my mind and I could not help but blurt out, "Tell me, Mayor Krag. You said that the Frankenstein castle has become the property of the government. Frankenstein bought it centuries ago. Does that mean it may still be purchased?"

'He turned away to look out the window at the distant hills. "Yes, it may still be." Suddenly, he snapped his head forward and stared at me. The twinkle that had once been in his eyes seemed to have been replaced by an angry fire. "But surely, Herr Winslow, you don't wish to imply...."

' "I wish to imply nothing," I told him quite matter-of-factly. "I only want to buy the place. How much is it?"

' "Castle Frankenstein," he stammered, "is not for sale."

'I grinned slyly. "But if the castle could be purchased once from the government, and no one wants the old place anyway, it can be purchased again."

'He shook his head.

' "N-no," he said.

'I began walking toward the door.

' "Then I will find out from the townspeople how to go about purchasing it."

'I turned back to see Krag's face become a mask of shock. He stood up from behind the desk and began walking toward me.

'*"Nein!"* he exclaimed. "You may buy the castle. Then leave my office and do not return. You are not welcome here. I only pray I am not doing something that I will later regret."

' "How much will it cost?"

'Mayor Krag quoted me a fair price for Castle Frankenstein, and almost immediately I had that exact amount in German currency in a neat stack upon his desk. Within minutes, the heavyset town official had prepared the deed to the castle. I

20

signed it, feeling a weird catharsis in the knowledge that I owned the very place that Frankenstein was supposed to have created his monster. I was soon to learn whether or not my theory was true concerning "Frankenstein". Please remember that everything I had heard thus far was only hearsay. But legends can be based on fact. I had to venture to the castle itself and see whether or not there was evidence that Frankenstein's unorthodox experiment was indeed reality.

'Reeling, I left the office of Mayor Krag with the signed document, and headed for my destination:

'CASTLE FRANKENSTEIN!

'The castle stood, as Krag had informed me, atop a hill overlooking Ingoldstadt. Its ancient spires and battlements still remained with a strength that could still withstand an attacking Medieval army. I felt a feeling of exhilaration as I stared up at the old, gothic structure, which now stood out against the night sky, its towers silhouetted against the large full moon with bizarre majesty. I tingled with the sudden thought that the castle might be filled with an aura of evil, momentarily sharing the superstitious fears of the townspeople. Then I stopped dreaming and again thought of my mission. I marveled as I stood beholding the very place where Victor Frankenstein might have created life. Beautiful in a grotesque sense, the castle was legally the property of Dr Burt Winslow.

'The old key which the Mayor had given me fit into the rusted lock. With a considerable amount of effort, I opened the ancient door with several good thrusts of my body against it. Again I was overcome by feelings of reverance and awe as I stepped into the dark interior of Castle Frankenstein. I may have been the first man to be within its walls in almost two hundred years.

'There was no illumination in the castle, except for the rays of the moon which streaked through the opened windows along with the whistling wind. I removed the flashlight from my pocket and sent a yellow beam streaming to the dank floor.

'The place was in complete shambles. Evidently, Victor Frankenstein was no housekeeper. The years that followed with their rain, dust, mold, and the like had further placed the castle in its current rundown condition. The whole place smelled from the dampness and decay of another age and reminded me of the foul rush of air that accompanies the opening of an ancient tomb. Still, the condition of the place was of no concern to me. This *was* Castle Frankenstein and that was all that mattered.

'Immediately I set out exploring, hoping to find some clues as to the truth of the creation of artificial life. After hardly walking any great distance, I came upon a very large chamber. Stepping into that chamber, I cast my flashlight beam upon what remained of an impressive set-up of apparatus and realised, to my utter delight, that I was actually standing in the laboratory of Victor Frankenstein.

'For a full minute I could do nothing but flash my beam in every conceivable direction, trying to see all that I could in the meager illumination. I finally regained my composure.

'The laboratory was not as elaborate or filled with gimmicks as you would expect, from watching those old and familiar Frankenstein motion pictures made in the 1930s and 1940s. Nevertheless, it was a scientific marvel even by today's standards. At first it was difficult to grasp that the laboratory was in use centuries ago. The equipment, though primitive, was more advanced than I had ever hoped imagine. Mary Shelley briefly passed over the scene in her novel wherein the monster came to life, implying that Victor had used a combination of galvanism and chemical injections to make his experiment. Now I knew for certain that Frankenstein indeed experimented in this laboratory and that he was familiar with the powers of electricity.

'Much of Frankenstein's equipment was damaged or corroded or both. The great engine that occupied a prominent place in the laboratory was beyond repair. The place was strewn with silky cobwebs. But I felt certain that, aided by my own twentieth century equipment and techniques, combined with Frankenstein's own secrets, I could easily set the laboratory into efficient operation once again.

'That was, if I could first locate the body of the monster.

'If the account of Mary Shelley was accurate enough, I knew that the monster was not to be found in Ingoldstadt. But again I am getting ahead of myself.

'In the center of the laboratory was a large table, complete with electrical hookups and large restraining straps which indicated that a giant man, over eight feet tall according to Mary

22

Shelley, might have been confined there.

'A warping bookcase was against one of the walls. Eagerly I pored through the volumes, hoping to come upon something scribed by Frankenstein himself. With a pounding heart, I discovered a treasury of scientific wealth – a great leather bound volume, written with a hasty hand, which chronicled the step-by-step creation of an artificial man, with the cover boasting in raised lettering *The Journal of Victor Frankenstein*. It was all there; how he violated the graves and the gallows, used even bits of animal tissue, how he worked for two years assembling a giant which he hoped to be virtuous, physically perfect, immune to disease, and the possessor of eternal life. He told how one night in November, the creature came to life, charged by the furies of an electrical storm and the power of his own devices. Reading the account was thoroughly invigorating.

'I began to fit the remaining pieces of the puzzle together, recalling what I could almost recite from memory from the novel *Frankenstein*. I noted that the account was told by Frankenstein to a Captain Walton, who had rescued him shortly before his death from the freezing wastes of the Arctic. Frankenstein was pursuing his creation, who had killed his lovely bride Elizabeth when the monster begged his maker to fashion him a mate, as hideous as himself, and was refused Victor chased his monster through Russia, across the Mediterranean Sea, and finally toward the North Pole. Captain Walton actually saw the monster after Frankenstein had died from overexposure to the elements. He saw the monster washed away on an ice flow, never to rise again to torment a world that had rejected it.

'Hastily, Captain Walton wrote down the story while Frankenstein had spoken in his delerium. There was good reason for some errors, which accounts for many of the discrepancies in the novel. Walton then turned over Victor's narrative, plus his own which served to frame the writing, to Mary Shelley, the wife of the poet Percy Bysshe Shelley, apparently hoping that her husband would write it into a gothic romance. She wrote the novel herself, added many of her own ideas to make the story read better as fiction, and the result is the most famous horror story of all time, *Frankenstein*.

'The important matter here is that I have proven that there was a Victor Frankenstein who, apparently, created a living man in a laboratory in Ingoldstadt. What remains is for me to prove the existence of that so-called monster and that it did, in fact, attain life.

'That, my friend, is to be the last phase of my adventure.'

Pierre Duré's face widened as Burt Winslow finished his narrative. He stared at the younger man intently, trying to decide whether or not he believed him.

'I told you you wouldn't believe my story,' said Winslow, crushing out the miniscule butt of his cigarette in the ashtray on the seat. 'You probably think I'm mad.'

The frenchman still looked puzzled.

'Mad?' he said. 'No, I don't think so. Somehow this madness all seems to make sense. Maybe I've been hypnotized by the train wheels or maybe I'm just gullible. But whatever, I believe you. Maybe I'm the one who's mad.'

Winslow laughed.

'But tell me Burt,' said Dupré, 'were you trying to tell me that you plan to . . . to . . .'

The scientist interrupted, 'Yes, I'm going to find – and revive – the Frankenstein monster.'

Dupré would not remain silent. 'The monster, though. I mean, wasn't the monster washed away in the Arctic? You must realize that the Arctic is quite a big place, my dear boy. You Americans have an old expression about finding a needle in a haystack. Well, how do you expect to find the monster?'

'According to Frankenstein's notes, the monster is immortal and can only be destroyed by some physical means, such as dissection or a big enough explosion. The cold of the Arctic should do little more than freeze him solid. With that understood, it is reasonable to assume that the monster still exists out there, encased in ice.'

'But you still haven't told me how you plan to find it.'

'Ah, you don't think I'd come this far without being prepared,' said Winslow with a grin, lighting another cigarette. 'When you have money it is easy to have people in other lands make investigations for you. I have, in this way, learned of a legend that has endured for almost two centuries among the eskimos of a certain area up North.'

'Legend?'

'There is some kind of mysterious Ice God that watches over these eskimos from an icy tomb.'

'An Ice God?' Dupré's eyes bulged in their sockets.

'A deity so hideous, so awesome, so enormous that no one dares to get near it. A god that has been there, never moving, but which, they believe, may one day emerge from the ice to unleash his terrible wrath upon his subjects. Sure, the natives have put their own embellishments into the story. But I believe that this Ice God, which keeps the eskimos in a grip of terror, is none other than the original Frankenstein monster.'

For a while Dupré could only stare into Winslow's face. No words followed and the American seemed to delight in the way he had startled his traveling companion. It was the conductor who interrupted the silence with the calling out the name of an obscure town.

'That's our stop,' said Winslow, eagerly standing up from the seat and reaching for his luggage.

CHAPTER 4

The Ravings of a Madman

The town which Dr Burt Winslow had entered was small, almost like a pioneer town of the American West. He and his French friend took in the scene. Horses, wagons and sleds seemed to be the main methods of transportation. Only a few automobiles moved along the snow-packed streets. The houses, with their snow covered roofs, were no closer than one hundred feet from each other.

There were a few stores about, including a general store where Winslow surmised he could purchase anything he would need for his expedition to the north. The back of the store served as myriad other functions, including a trading post, assay office, and post office.

A medical center, indeed a small hospital, was at the far end of one street. It was, Winslow later learned, mostly run by educated eskimos and had many of the facilities of any modern hospital.

Down and across the street was a rather average sized building with an adjoining garage.

Burt Winslow stood still for a moment, deep in thought.

'I really need you on this trip, Pierre.'

'Ah! And for that reason, nothing will drag me away. I'd have been bored spending my vacation at a communications base anyway. Monsters are far more exciting!'

The Frenchman was laughing so hard that clouds of visible breath issued from his mouth.

'If not for me,' he said, 'you might be forced to try and

hire some help among the natives. And from what you've told me about their legendary Ice God, I doubt you'd have much luck. They might even give you some trouble. Superstitious people usually do not stand for their deity being taken from them. Luckily I am a good shot with both pistol and rifle, in case we encounter any trouble.'

'Thank you,' said Winslow, walking faster. 'I'll need you. Mr Lamont runs a one-man operation here. So I doubt he'll be able to get away and leave things all locked up. I don't doubt you about the native help. We'll probably be the entire hunting party, Pierre. Just you and I . . . and, of course, the Frankenstein monster.'

The two travelers stopped in front of the Morris Lamont Transport company and looked toward the garage. The door was partially open and they could see that two large trucks waited within.

They walked into the office of the company, tracking in trails of snow that quickly melted with the warmth of the many radiators. No one seemed to be about and so Winslow tapped a bell on the service counter.

A few seconds later, they heard a gruff voice from the back of the store.

'Yes, sirs, may I help you, sirs?'

Winslow looked up at the worn, whiskered face of the man approaching him from the other side of the counter.

'Mr Lamont?'

'That's me,' he said with little inflection. 'You want to do business here?'

'My name is Winslow. Dr Burt Winslow. I had written you last month about reserving dogsled and a truck. I hope you remember me.'

'Of course, I remember, Dr Winslow. It's all set to go, just as you wanted,' Lamont ran his hand across his sandpaper beard. 'But tell me, doctor. Why do you want both a sled and a truck? Why not just one or the other?'

'Simple,' said the scientist. 'I want to go to an area where it would be impossible to get a truck in and out. But I'm after something too big to take all the way by dogsled. No use taking the sled all the way, either, when we can use the truck up to a point. It is quite far, you see, that I'll be going.'

27

'Then be a little more particular, said Lamont. 'Tell me more of your method.'

'We drive the truck in as far as we can with the dogsled inside,' Winslow said, talking with his hands tying to describe the scene. 'When we can't go any further by truck, we take out the sled and dogs, hitch them up, ride out to the end of the line, bring what we came for back to the truck, and drive away. Simple, isn't it?'

'Yes, doctor, only for one thing,' answered Lamont. 'Something I've been wanting to know ever since I got your letter last month. Just what is this thing that you're trying to bring back? I can't think of anything of value up in those wastes.'

Winslow looked hard into Lamont's face, anticipating his shock when he told him, 'The sacred Ice God of the eskimos.'

'The Ice God!' exclaimed Lamont, loud enough to be heard outside. 'But you can't be serious, doctor. You don't really believe those fanatical stories, do you? Sure, I've heard some tales about a tomb of ice up there and some Ice God scaring all the natives. But nobody in his right mind would believe any of them.'

'I assure you Dr Winslow is in his right mind,' said Dupré defensively.

'It's all right, Pierre,' Winslow said, looking at him momentarily. 'But it's not a matter of what you believe, Mr Lamont. It's what I believe and what you are getting paid for my little expedition.'

'I guess you're right, doctor,' he said, bowing his head and laughing to himself. 'Money's money. And if you want to waste yours, that's your business.'

'Well,' said Winslow, 'maybe I won't be wasting it. We'll just have to wait and see.'

Morris Lamont's mind rambled for a few moments before speaking again.

'You know, doctor,' he said matter-of-factly, 'right now in our little hospital is a man who claims he was back there, in that taboo area of the natives. Said he saw some kind of a monster or demon frozen in the ice.'

Winslow's eyebrows shot upward.

'Did you say *monster*?'

'Yeah,' Lamont went on without emotion. 'Of course the guy was a raving lunatic. Drunk to the gills too, I might add, and delerious from the cold.'

'What!' Winslow burst from his state of speechlessness. 'What's this you're talking about? A man says he saw . . . Was he a native?'

'No, an Englishman. In fact, it was I who found him. I was transporting some pelts in one of my sleds when I saw him lying out there in the snow, mostly dead. Half froze, he was, and babbling about seeing something horrible in the ice. He pointed toward that sacred tomb territory, then passed out. He smelled like a keg of whiskey too.'

'This is more than I could have hoped for!' said Winslow loudly. 'Go on, man. Anything else?'

Winslow glowered with excitement. He had never even hoped to obtain such a clue to the monster's icy tomb. But the doctor had to verify the story.

'There were human footprints and sled marks all around the area where I found him,' said Lamont. 'It had stopped snowing so the tracks stayed there for a while. Now that seemed strange to me. Seems like someone came by there and left him to die in the snow.'

'You didn't see the Ice God yourself?' asked Dupré.

Lamont shook his head.

'Not me,' he said. 'Nothing like any Ice God that I could see.'

'If he saw the Ice God,' said Winslow authoritatively, 'it's possible that he was discovered, taken away, and dumped where you found him, by those natives who worship it. You know, as a kind of punishment for defiling their sacred land.'

'Exactly how I figured it,' answered Lamont. 'Of course, the crazy antics of a few natives don't convince me there really is anything out there. A drunk freezing to death can see anything, I suppose.'

'I suppose,' Winslow repeated.

'And you say this man,' started Pierre Dupré who had been remarkably silent, 'is in the hospital at this very moment?'

'That's right,' said Lamont. 'He was at the medical center last I heard. And judging from his condition, he's not going anywhere for a while.'

'Burt, of course we'll talk to this man right away,' said Dupré anxiously.

'Of course,' said the scientist turning toward the door. 'We're on our way already.'

29

The two men left their luggage on the floor and bolted for the door of the office. Then they stopped to look back at Lamont.

'Get everything prepared, Mr Lamont,' said Winslow. 'We leave early tomorrow morning. Come on, Pierre. To the medical center!'

'He sounds as crazy as that guy in the hospital,' said Morris Lamont as Burt Winslow and the Frenchman rushed from his office and toward the medical center.

A middle-aged native doctor greeted Winslow and his friend at the main desk of the hospital.

'Of course, you may see Mr Fairfax,' the physician said. 'He's coming along fine. But I fear I must warn you.'

'Warn me?' asked Winslow.

'Mr Fairfax cannot be taken too seriously. He was raving when we brought him in here. And quite intoxicated. The whiskey probably saved his life out there in that cold, because by all rights he should have been dead.'

'He can talk to us, can't he?'

'Yes, Dr Winslow. But like I said, he rants and raves about a lot of ridiculous things I could never accept.'

'And how is the patient?' asked Winslow.

'Physically, well, he'll be under our care for a while yet. His legs suffered frostbite.'

'Hmmm,' said the scientist, dispelling from his mind any thoughts for a possible third member of the expedition.

'Please do not excite him,' said the physician.

'I'll try not to, doctor. And now will you please lead us to his room?'

'Certainly,' said the eskimo doctor, leading Winslow and Dupré down the hall and into a private room.

The hospital room was clean but nothing elaborate. Light streaked inside the room through the drawn venetian blinds. In the center of the room, a man lay upon a bed under the spotless, white hospital linens. The bedridden man's eyes looked up as the two foreign visitors approached his bed.

'Some visitors to see you Mr Fairfax,' said the doctor, motioning with his hand to step forward. 'They want to talk to you about what you saw.'

Fairfax gazed at the two men. His eyes were like watery

sockets, his mouth forming a frown that advertised his contempt for them.

'The monster!' he exclaimed, motioning violently from the bed until the pain in his legs forced him to remain motionless. He saw in them only two more people to make him the fool, the drunken clown who claimed to have seen a demon in the ice. Here were more spectators to see the show, he thought.

Winslow and Dupré exchanged glances.

'No!' shouted Fairfax, groaning from the pain of tormented legs. 'No more about the monster! I've had enough! I'll not be anyone's personal freak show anymore! Get them out of here!'

'Please calm down, Mr Fairfax,' cautioned the physician.

Then Winslow interrupted, speaking in a kind voice, 'But you don't understand, Mr Fairfax.'

'Don't understand? What's there to understand? You're like all the others. You want to make fun out of me like everyone else around here. To laugh at me.'

Winslow's handsome face showed complete honesty.

'We're not going to laugh at you,' he said.

'Then why are you here?' Fairfax hollered. 'No, get out! If you want to see a show, find a circus. But leave me alone!'

'But at least let me explain our motives,' returned Winslow, determined and maintaining a sincere smile. 'I'm here because I believe you.'

'You? Believe me?'

Fairfax found it impossible to believe those words. No one had believed him yet. Why should anyone believe him now?

'And why would you believe me?' he asked, his eyes almost crying.

No one noticed the eskimo intern who happened to pass the doorway at that moment. Unseen, he paused just outside the door long enough for him to mentally photograph the two strangers. His lip wrinkled into a cruel frown. Then he vanished down the corridor.

'Why don't you think I'm crazy like everyone else does?' asked the patient.

Winslow turned toward the physician.

'Do you mind leaving us alone with the patient?' he asked. 'Just for a short time. I think we'll learn more from him if we're alone. We can talk freer then. I promise we'll try not to rile him up.'

'All right,' said the doctor, 'but don't be too long.' He walked out of the room. Dupré closed the door behind him.

Burt Winslow leaned over the bed and looked Fairfax sternly in the eyes.

'I'll come to the point, Mr Fairfax,' he said. 'I understand you saw this Ice God that has had the natives scared all these years. Please answer me. It's extremely important.'

Somehow, at last, Fairfax believed Winslow. It seemed obvious to the bedridden man that Winslow was not about to deride him. For the first time since they entered his room, Fairfax felt at ease.

'Ice God!' he said. 'That's what they call it. Well, let me tell you that what I saw was no god. It was a demon! Or a monster out of hell!'

Winslow believed in getting to the point. 'Then I'd appreciate it very much if you would describe this . . . this demon, as you call it.'

'Ah, now there I'll have no trouble,' said Fairfax, his eyes glowing like lights. He was no longer hesitant to speak. 'Well, this creature or monster or whatever it was that I saw was big, huge. A giant.'

'About eight feet tall?' asked Winslow.

'Taller, considering the high boots it was wearing.'

Winslow whispered to Dupré, 'Checks out so far.'

'Well, this was a giant,' Fairfax continued. 'But that wasn't the worst of it. Its face, ugh! if that's what you want to call it, was monstrous. Horrible. I'll never forget that face as long as I live. It was the most revolting thing I have ever seen and doubt that I'll ever see anything worse.'

'Can you give me some details?' asked Winslow.

Fairfax swallowed hard, his face distorting as he recalled the countenance of the thing that had stared at him from the glassy prison of ice. Evidently he still feared the creature.

'The demon was utterly monstrous,' said Fairfax, wincing over the recollection. 'The arms looked too long for the body. They reminded me of the stretched arms of a mummy. They stuck out of the torn sleeves, ripped up to the elbows. And the hands. The hands were enormous, with deep gashes in the flesh and crude stitches apparently holding them together.'

'What of the face?' asked the scientist, moving closer to Fairfax.

'The face was the worst of all,' Fairfax went on.

As Fairfax spoke, Winslow seemed to be making mental calculations. He continued to whisper to Dupré.

'The flesh was yellow, very pale, like Death itself. The hair was black, long, hanging to its massive shoulders. And I'll never forget all those scars and stitches. There were these two things that seemed like metal bolts sticking out of the head. I saw them only a few moments before I passed out. I'm not sure what that creature was in the ice. But this I'll swear to – it was no god!'

Winslow's face was illuminated like a torch. Turning again to Dupré, he exclaimed, 'It's got to be, Pierre! The timing, the description, everything is too perfect for it to be anything else!'

'Be what?' asked the confused Fairfax, trying to sit up in the bed. 'What are you talking about? You seem to know more about this demon than I do.'

'I won't keep you in the dark any longer, Mr Fairfax,' said Winslow, smiling. 'After what you've been through and told us, you certainly deserve it. What we, Mr Dupré and I, believe that you saw is . . . '

'Yes?'

'The Frankenstein monster!'

Fairfax stared at Winslow incredulously. 'The Frankenstein monster?' he repeated with disbelief. He scratched his head, starting to believe that the men who were standing before his bed were madder than he ever could be. 'But, I mean . . . There's no such thing, is there? The Frankenstein monster is an imaginary character, isn't it? A monster from the cinema and American comic books? Boris Karloff and all that?'

'I'm afraid not,' Winslow said, explaining briefly about his involvement with the subject of Frankenstein. 'Can you tell us where this block of ice is, Mr Fairfax?'

'Yes, it's simple. My plane is still out there in that embankment. I doubt the eskimos have dragged that hulk away,' he laughed. There is only one open door in the ship. I may have been intoxicated, but I'm certain I walked relatively perpendicular away from that door. Keep going in that general direction and you won't help but see that white monolith rising out of the snow. Follow those directions and you'll have your Ice God or the Frankenstein monster.'

'And how do we find the plane, monsieur?' asked Dupré.

'That too is simple,' answered Fairfax. 'Just go off in the direction of the so-called sacred tomb and you'll hit it.'

'Thank you very much, Mr Fairfax,' said Winslow, storming out of the room with a trail of cigarette smoke in his wake.

'Hey, just a minute,' Fairfax started.

But Winslow and Dupré did not hear him. They were already leaving the hospital, planning the morning's schedule, and anticipating the journey that would bring them face to unsightly face with what they hoped to be Frankenstein's immortal monster.

CHAPTER 5

Death in the Shadows

The clock said it was evening. Yet the afternoon sun still shone brightly in this cold land at the top of the world where nights and days lasted for six months each.

Pierre Dupré wished it were really night. Still, he was used to sleeping while the sun still beamed through the slits in his venetian blinds. The journey on the train had exhausted him and he was glad to sleep in a real bed for a change. This was his first real opportunity to rest since he met Burt Winslow. He set the alarm clock to awaken him a few hours before he and the scientist were to set off on their quest. The hotel that he and Winslow had stopped in was peaceful and he felt assured that his sleep would not be disturbed.

On the other hand, Winslow was too excited to sleep. He tossed for a while, contorting himself in the bed, but was not in the least tired. Soon he was on his feet and pacing the floor, with thoughts of castles and graverobbing and mad experiments flooding his mind. Slumber was impossible, he finally agreed. He could think only of the following day's activities.

He walked the length of the room several times, then the width, then the length again. His bare feet silently paced the rug so that anyone outside might have thought him asleep.

Winslow was first aware of the intruder when he heard the faint sound of metal tinkling against metal from the door lock.

Cautiously, Winslow turned to face the door, hearing the sound that told him someone was tampering with the lock. He surmised that a poorly made skeleton key had been placed into the lock. Finally he observed that the doorknob was turning. The door began to slowly open. The scientist silently sprang to press his back against the wall, out of the line of vision of the intruder.

Panther like, the intruder prowled into the room. Winslow could see that he was rather stout, wore a handkerchief mask over his face, and clutched a dagger with an ominous, gleaming blade. The doctor watched him as he stealthily crept toward the bed where the piled blankets suggested a sleeping man. He raised the dagger and suddenly realized what he had mistaken to be his prey but it was too late. Winslow had already leaped upon his back.

First, in a blinding motion, Winslow seized the dagger from his would-be killer's hand. The weapon dropped to the floor. Catching the intruder off guard, Winslow spun him around only to have two steel like hands grip him about the throat, squeezing, forcing him to gag. But the doctor was in the peak of physical condition. Without hesitation, he brought his knee up crashing hard into the intruder's chest, sending him reeling backwards, moaning from the pain, into the bed.

Winslow flew into space and onto the stunned masked man. Frantic hands tore the handkerchief from his face. Winslow stared into the hate-filled face of an eskimo whom he had glimpsed briefly in the halls of the hospital.

'You shall never reach the Ice God!' the eskimo snarled.

Again his hands were around Winslow's throat.

Once more the scientist tried to free himself from being choked to death. He tugged, pulling himself and his assailant off the bed and onto the floor. In the conflict Winslow managed to return to his feet and slam a rock hard fist into the eskimo's face, just as the sound of footsteps filled the room.

The eskimo, his jaw red from the blow, took advantage of the confusion and sprang to his feet as Winslow turned his head toward the door to see Dupré and the irate hotel manager gawking at him. With a blur of action, the assailant was again reaching for the dagger.

'No, you don't!' shouted the doctor, bashing him in the face, the stomach, and again in the face.

The native fell to the floor unconscious as Dupré called Winslow's name.

'What's going on in here?' demanded the angry manager of

the hotel. 'Are you trying to wreck my place?'

'If there is any damage I'll pay for it,' offered Winslow, noting that there was nothing broken that he could detect, except, perhaps, the native's jaw. He tossed the manager a bundle of dollar bills, which sent him trotting from the room with a silly grin on his face.

'Pierre,' said Burt Winslow, rubbing his throat which bore the red imprints where his assailant had choked him, 'we had better call the police.'

Pierre Dupré looked shocked.

Winslow, on the other hand, resolved himself to the fact that he should expect more trouble in the morning.

CHAPTER 6

The Ice God

Castle Frankenstein stood like a monstrous, stone gargoyle against Ingoldstadt's blue sky. The only sounds were made by chirping birds that had made their nests in an opening in one of the towers and the noise made by rotating wagon wheels. The wagon was driven by a haggard looking man who fiercely cracked the whip over the horse that drew him and his passenger up to the door of the castle.

'You sure this is where you want me to let you off, *frauline*?' he asked in a gruff voice, squinting at the awesome structure built during the middle ages. A sly grin curled his lips for he knew that no other man in Ingoldstadt would have driven her to the dreaded castle of Frankenstein. 'You know what place this is.'

'I know perfectly well,' the girl replied, handing him a generous payment for her wagon ride.

The driver scratched his curly hair, then jumped down from the wagon. He could not justify her being at the castle. Surely a beautiful young woman could not possibly ask to be driven to Castle Frankenstein.

The girl's beauty was pure, youthful. She appeared to be barely twenty-one years old. As the driver helped her off the wagon, he could see her perfect figure and felt the firmness of her trim waist. She stepped to the ground with her clothes flattering her every curve and her long, blonde hair billowing in the gentle breeze.

The driver removed her luggage from the waggon, then took

his place behind the horse. He again cracked the whip and the wagon rolled away from the castle, over the bridge which crossed the river, heading back toward the town where he was eager to help propagate the gossip about a beautiful woman who had come to the despised Frankenstein castle.

For a while Lynn Powell could only stand and marvel at the once proud fortress. She had never before seen a castle except in pictures and the new experience was positively enthralling. Her golden hair, which flowed nearly to her waist, moved in the breeze and caressed her shoulders.

Lynn walked to the castle door, noticing the five enormous wooden crates stamped FRAGILE waiting on the patio. Although she knew the nature of those crates, she mechanically read the tags to herself.

'To: Dr Burt Winslow. Paid.'

'Burt's equipment arrived,' she thought, 'or at least the first shipment. I'd better leave all of this out here until Burt gets back here.'

The door to Castle Frankenstein seemed strong enough to keep out an army in its day. The door was constructed of strong wood and rose high above her. Strips of rusted, bolted metal braced it to give it added strength. Some of the timbers were warped out of shape. The new lock which Winslow had put onto the door gleamed shiny in the bright sunlight and appeared to be anachronistic with the door itself.

The girl anxiously searched her purse and found the key which Winslow had entrusted to her. She held it tightly, her heart pounding rapidly, then slid the key into the brand new lock. She twisted it and opened the great door to the legendary castle.

Flicking on the switch to the electric lights which Winslow had installed, Lynn Powell walked through the castle, her eyes wide with awe. The electric light hardly did anything for the place except to accent its extreme delapidation. Winslow had obviously done nothing to remove any of the signs of age and decay, other than knocking down most of the spider and cobwebs.

Lynn paused, wondering how long the building had stood atop that hill before Victor Frankenstein had moved into it. Then she went outside and brought in her suitcases.

There was little for her to do at this point. Winslow had only

given her an estimation when he would be returning to Ingoldstadt. Lynn was not the type of woman who preferred staying
home and performing the established womanly chores. But for
lack of anything better to do to occupy the long hours and days
that followed, she resolved to make Castle Frankenstein look
more the way she assumed a castle should look.

The large truck with the MORRIS LAMONT TRANSPORT
CO. lettering painted on its canvas covering rumbled out of
the garage like a surplus World War II tank. It thundered, black
smoke coughing out of the smokestack near the driver's cab,
along the snow flecked road. Exhust fumes billowed into the
cold Arctic air.

Three men sat in the cab of the canvas topped truck. The
driver, Morris Lamont, occasionally took one hand off the
steering wheel to rub the stubble on his face. Next to him sat
Dr Burt Winslow, who tried to remain calm although he had
been hypertense ever since his encounter with the would-be
killer in his hotel room. By the other window was the Frenchman, Pierre Dupré, who was again chewing on an empty pipe.

Behind the cab, under the canvas covering of the vehicle,
dogs continuously barked.

'And that man who attacked me was proven to definitely be
an intern from the hospital,' said Winslow.

'But now he's in jail where he belongs,' said Dupré. 'Fanatics
can be terribly dangerous, you know. He could have killed you,
Burt.'

'Probably would have, if not for Lamont's six months of daylight keeping me up all night.'

Morris Lamont turned away from the windshield, which
showed hardly anything more than the bleak whiteness of snow
and ice, and snickered at his two passengers. 'My six month
sun? My friends, you can take it back with you when you leave
here.'

'That man who tried to kill me must have overheard us talking to Fairfax in the hospital,' continued Winslow. 'Obviously
the natives aren't too happy about our trying to find their Ice
God. He must have followed us back to the hotel and found out
my room number.'

'It's a good thing you told the police to watch Fairfax's bed,'
said Dupré. 'Now that it's gotten out that he told us what he

did, his life will be in constant danger.'

Lamont continued driving on the course outlined by Fairfax. He was glad that he had decided to come along on the trip and not remain back at the shipping company office. Business was slow anyway these days and Lamont liked nothing better than an excuse to get away from the place.

As he listened to Winslow and Dupré converse, he constantly watched the great extants of whiteness, carefully scrutinizing every bit of movement that contrasted against the snow.

'Those superstitious natives are a funny lot,' he said. 'But we'd better watch out for them. I wouldn't be surprised if they started something even if we do have a monstrous truck like this. Remember that we're going into their sacred grounds. Can you imagine what so-called civilized men in the United States would do, Dr Winslow, if some characters went in there and stole their altar or something?'

'I know,' said Winslow. 'In their eyes we'll be persecutors of their faith. That's why I had you bring along those rifles.'

'You had me bring enough guns to hold off a regiment,' said Lamont.

'I hope it isn't necessary to use them,' answered the scientist.

'We just might have to,' replied the driver sternly, scanning the bleak horizon.

The truck continued to speed over the monotonous white land with the road gradually diminishing to a snow-padded track. The wind was blowing harder against the canvas of the truck and caused the dogs to become even more restless.

The truck's cab heater offered only meager protection from the cold. The two men seated next to the driver repeatedly rubbed themselves to get their blood moving faster. But it was the anticipation of what they would hopefully find that really made them forget much of their discomfort.

There were no other vehicles in the area that any of the three men could see. No people, no animals, or anything save the great snowy mounds which surrounded the truck, that seemed so dwarfed by the northern scenery.

Without warning, after a considerable trek across the white wastes, Morris Lamont cleared his raspy voice and applied his foot to the brake. The mammoth truck thundered to a halt, slipping a bit on the glossy strip that served as a road.

'This is as far as we can take the truck,' said Lamont, looking out over the Arctic desolation.

'That's why the dogs, Mr Lamont,' said Winslow.

'And from the sound of them back there,' said Dupré, 'I'd say they'll be glad to get out of the truck. They've been couped up in there for quite a while.'

'Well, let's get moving then,' said Winslow, not wanting to waste a precious second. 'Mr Lamont, will you please wait here and guard the truck while Pierre and I go off on the sleds?'

'Sure,' answered Lamont. 'You don't think I'm going to leave this valuable truck out here, do you? Especially not with angry eskimos lurking behind every icicle!'

'Thank you again,' Mr Lamont,' said the doctor politely, 'for coming out here with us.'

Lamont shook his head and waved.

'Aww, go on,' he said. 'Nothing at all. Anyway, you paid me enough for this little trip so I won't need another client all month.'

Dupré opened the door of the truck and he and Winslow stepped out into the cold. Fighting the sudden rush of freezing air that bit into their faces, they hurried to the back of the truck, their boots digging into the snow. They donned the snowshoes which Winslow had purchased at the general store, then slushed awkwardly about, removed the ramp from the truck, and attached it to the rear.

Dupré took the two loaded rifles while Winslow ran up the ramp and entered the truck, where he hitched up the teams of huskies. He had rented a second team and sled with the addition of Dupré to the team. Dupré re-checked the rest of the gear and made certain that the axes, picks, hooks, shovels, and varied tools were all securely wrapped in their supply packs.

Within minutes, the dogs and the sled were waiting for Winslow and Dupré to cry *mush*.

Both Winslow and the Frenchman took their places on the sleds, nodded to one another, and shouted 'Mush!' with a crack of the whip. The huskies immediately pulled on their burdens. Winslow turned slightly to see Lamont waving at him from the parked truck, then saw it disappear in the snowy distance.

Neither of the men could escape the feeling that they were being spied upon by hate filled eyes. They maintained a constant watch as they drove the dogs harder and faster through the winderness. The wind assaulted them with more force than ever and it was almost impossible to breathe.

Suddenly Winslow's eyes snapped and a look of utter enlightenment swept over his handsome face. In the distance he perceived a large flash of silver reflecting in the sunlight. As his dogs drew him nearer to the flash he could identify the tail end of an airplane.

'There!' he shouted to Dupré, releasing one hand from the reins and pointing. 'The plane! Fairfax's crashed plane!'

Dupré saw the ship and nodded in acknowledgment. He tried to yell back to Winslow but his voice would not carry over the yelping and barking of his dogs.

'We know that so far Fairfax was telling the truth!' Winslow cried.

The two dogsleds proceeded in the direction told them by Fairfax. The sweeping wind no longer seemed to matter; nor did the stinging coldness of the men's faces. They forced the dogs to pull them faster until there, standing up from the snow like some frozen gravestone, was a peculiar block of ice, reflecting the sun almost like a snow-flecked mirror.

'Over there!' roared Winslow, pointing.

Both of them stared at the upright piece of ice as the dogs drew nearer to it. They perceived the dark area that betrayed the fact that there was, indeed, something imprisoned in that ice. As they came steadily closer to the frozen block, they noticed that the shadowy figure was that of a large, manlike creature.

They knew that it could be nothing else than the Ice God.

Fired by enthusiasm, both of them reined their dogsleds to a halt.

'Do you think – ?' Dupré began.

Winslow interrupted, 'I don't think, Pierre! I know!'

'Then come on and let's get up there!' exclaimed Dupré.

Taking their packs of equipment, their rifles and pistols with them, the two explorers hastened to the block of ice. The dogs were barking behind them as Winslow rushed to the darkened form. It had snowed since Fairfax had been there and a layer of snow now covered much of the glassy object. Like two madmen, their hearts nearly erupting with enthusiasm, Winslow and Dupré brushed aside the snow. Then they stepped back, gasping, taking in the biting air.

Before them, peering out from the block of ice, was the giant creature, its hating face snarling down at them as if from a frozen mask of horror.

'It's . . . it is,' Dupré began, but found himself too speechless to proceed. He could only look in wonder and hope that Winslow would speak in his stead.

'Yes, Pierre,' said Winslow, surprisingly subdued, 'it's the Frankenstein monster.' Then he stared at the hideous creature in silent reverance, as if it surely were a god.

'Come on, then,' said Dupré, taking a pick in his hand and gripping it tightly. 'Let's start chopping away the ice so we can get the monster back to the truck.'

Winslow snapped out of his trance-like state.

'Yes!' he agreed. 'We'll chop away just enough of the ice to get it back by dogsled. But not too much of the ice. I don't want it thawing out on us.'

'Thawing out?' asked Dupré with curiosity. 'What does that matter? It's dead, isn't it?'

Winslow shook his head, a serious look on his face.

'If Victor Frankenstein really did make his creation immortal, then don't think for a moment that it is dead. The beast could revive on us. But I don't want that to happen till I've taken all the precautions I need. And when he revives, it will be the way that I want him to. Therefore, the monster stays dormant until I get it back to Ingoldstadt.'

'But why do you need laboratory equipment to revive him, then? Can't you just thaw him out whenever you want?'

'I cannot say. To revive him now would produce a weakling, most likely. Remember how long he's been in that ice. You see, I want the monster to come back as Frankenstein intended him – by recreating Victor's experiment in his own castle.'

'Well, even if it did come to life, we have guns,' said Dupré, confidently smacking the butt of his rifle.

'I doubt if guns would have too much effect on him,' replied Winslow. 'No, let's do it my way. All right? Now we'd better start chopping before we have to use those guns on some of the local populace.'

Like children opening a giant Christmas present, Burt Winslow and Pierre Dupré began to chip and slash away the ice. Bits and chunks of ice flew about in all directions as they worked, always careful not to strike the monster with their tools. The minutes passed as the two men feverishly removed more and more of the confining ice. Neither winced as small, frozen particles shot into their faces. They were making steady progress, which was all that mattered.

But even while they chopped the ice, they heard the sound of dogs, not their own, coming from the opposite direction. Winslow and his friend stopped chopping and turned to see the dark dots moving across the reaches of snow.

'That's why we have rifles!' said Winslow.

'The eskimos!' exclaimed Dupré, noticing the parkas of the small band of men approaching them by dogsled. 'They left Fairfax to die just for seeing their deity.'

'And here we are, trying to steal it!'

They stopped their nearly finished task of chopping out the monster. Winslow snatched up his rifle. A bullet streaked over his head, piercing the upper edge of what remained of the ice block. The eskimos had left their sleds.

'They've got guns this time, Pierre!' he called out to the Frenchman. 'If you can keep chopping and get the monster out, I'll cover you. Don't worry, I was –'

'I know. You were top man on the university's shooting team.'

'Something like that. But keep at the ice. The job is almost done anyway. I won't have to hold them off too long.'

Winslow stood in front of his partner, using his body to shield both Pierre and the monster. The Frenchman kept hammering away at the ice while bullets continued to echo and whiz overhead. A shot nearly creased Winslow's fur lined hood.

'Hurry, Pierre! That was *too* close!'

'I'm going as fast as I can, monsieur!'

Winslow aimed his weapon and fired. An armed eskimo fell into the snow, staining it with his blood. Dupré tried not to look, even though a bullet might at any moment come ripping into his back. He kept on working, letting most of what remained of the ice that was to be removed fall to the snow.

Again, again, the eskimos blasted at the invaders with their firearms. Luckily they were poor shots and Winslow was agile enough to keep moving out of their range of fire.

Winslow fired again. A second native moaned and plunged face first into the snow.

'Hurry, Pierre! There are more of them coming! If they

should rush us or make for our dogs . . . '

The air was alive with the sounds of barking dogs and bullets. Shards of ice flew from the impact of hot bullets as well as from Dupré's smashing axe.

Then Winslow heard the words that he had been waiting for, shouted over the cacophony of noise.

'Burt! I've done it!'

'Finished? Great work,' said the scientist, still firing his weapon and evading the barrage of bullets, any of which could have ended his quest in a moment. 'Quick, now! Slide it along to the dogsleds and attach it with those grappling hooks. But make it fast. I can't keep holding them off. There are too many of them. Thought I could but – !'

He dashed aside to avoid another bullet as Dupré shoved the frozen monster, toppling it back into the snow. Winslow followed him, firing his rifle rapidly until it clicked empty. He dropped the useless weapon and removed his pistol from its holster and continued to blast away at the natives, striking two of them in the heart and maintaining a cover for Dupré. Burt saw his partner attach the grappling hooks to the monster.

'All right, Burt! We can drag it away from here!'

'Okay, then let's get away!'

Shooting down another eskimo, Winslow rushed to his dogsled, the one with the frozen carcass of the Frankenstein monster attached to the back. The eskimos had been reduced in their numbers by half, but their losses did not diminish their determination.

Whips cracked. Dogs barked. Winslow, Dupré, and the frozen monster began sliding across the snow.

The weight of the frozen giant slowed down Winslow's dogsled considerably. Yet he managed to drain the maximum output from the animals. They had already gained a good start as the eskimos returned to their sleds and went after the thieves in fast pursuit.

'Faster, Pierre!' shouted Winslow, looking back to check that the grappling hooks were holding the monster and seeing the approaching horde of natives. 'Faster!'

Winslow saw that Dupré was gaining on him, his sled's speed not impaired by the added weight. The eskimo's sleds were coming uncomfortably close to Winslow and Dupré. And there seemed to be no letting up of their gunfire.

Both of them sighed with relief to see Lamont's truck waiting in the distance. Lamont, aroused from the truck by the sounds of shooting and the sight of the dogsleds, stood in the snow. There was a rifle in his hand and as the chase neared the truck, Lamont joined in the battle. More eskimos fell and bullets ricocheted off the truck.

Both Winslow and Dupré pulled their sleds alongside the truck. Dupré and Lamont instinctively slid the dogs and the sleds up the ramp of the truck, then did the same with the monster, while Winslow never stopped firing. He grabbed two of the additional rifles from the vehicle and felt confident that he would not run out of ammunition before his attackers would.

As Dupré and Lamont finished their work and dropped the canvas over the back of the truck, Winslow called to them.

'All right! Get inside the truck! I'll follow you!'

Lamont rushed around the front of the truck, the sheer mass of the vehicle protecting him from the bullets. The other eskimos, observing his tactics, moved around the front of the truck. For a few moments, Dupré seemed confused, not knowing which door to enter.

'Get inside, Pierre!' commanded the scientist, firing his rifle.

Without further delay, Dupré rushed to the other door. As he began to climb into the truck, an eskimo's bullet tore into him. Blood splattered upon the door of the truck as Winslow reacted with horror.

'Pierre!' he shouted, then turned to place a bullet through the skull of the man who had shot his friend.

Winslow rushed to his friend, ignoring the bullets that bounced from the truck only inches away from his own head, and dragged him inside the cab.

Pierre moaned, clutching his arm.

'I'll live, Burt,' he said. 'J-just my shoulder. But it sure hurts.'

There was no longer any reason to fire. Lamont gunned the accelerator of the truck and they were soon driving away from what remained of the vengeful horde. As Winslow realized that the eskimos were at a safe distance behind them, he wiped a river of sweat from his brow that had formed there despite the freezing cold.

CHAPTER 7

Departure

Burt Winslow, Pierre Dupré, and Morris Lamont all sat in a back room of the latter's business establishment. The room was filled with cold air, as Winslow had felt it best to keep the radiators shut off for the present. The three men sat before the large form of the Frankenstein monster, covered with a thick layer of ice, which was the reason for the coldness of the room. They rubbed their arms to keep warm.

There was a slight puddle of water beneath the frozen Frankenstein monster. But there was no real danger of the creature thawing out as long as the radiators remained shut off. The fist of the monster was still raised as if the patchwork horror were waiting to catch them all off guard and strike at them with its superhuman strength.

'I still find it difficult to believe,' marveled Pierre Dupré, chewing on his cold pipe. One of his arms was fixed rigidly in a sling. 'To think that we are looking at the actual corpse of the Frankenstein monster.'

'Er, not corpse, Pierre,' Winslow corrected. 'Remember?'

'I'm sorry, Burt. I mean body. The monster, you say, cannot die.'

Lamont's jaw dropped open.

'What!' he interjected. 'You mean to say that this *thing* is alive?'

'That's right,' said Winslow. 'The monster was imprisoned in this ice but I believe it never died. It cannot die by ordinary means. In fact, even though it cannot move or feel at this

48

moment, it is probably more alive than any of us here, It's in suspended animation and can be made to walk again.'

Lamont looked worried and started to reach for his pistol.

'Well, if that thing comes to while I'm sitting here, I want to be prepared.'

'No need to worry about that,' said Winslow confidently, 'when we start those radiators to thaw him out.'

'What?' both Lamont and Dupré exclaimed simultaneously.

'You're going to melt that ice?' added Lamont. 'You can't be serious.'

'Don't worry,' he laughed, 'I'm fully prepared to cope with the monster if he thaws out. Remember, he'll probably be in a weakened condition after being in that ice for so long.'

'Probably?' said Dupré.

Winslow walked to the back of the room and returned with a leather object. He held it out so that Dupré and Lamont could examine it.

'A gas mask,' said Lamont.

'Yes,' Winslow began to explain, 'if the monster should revive, I'll simply clamp that mask over his face and give it enough gas to put an elephant to sleep. I have enough gas to keep the Monster out cold for several trips the length of the one we'll be taking.'

'Well, I hope it works,' said Lamont, 'for all of our sakes.' The owner of the transport company could not feel easy in the presence of the monster regardless of his growing familiarity with the brute.

'Shall we start the heaters?' asked Winslow.

Before too long, the room was warmed by the radiators and a crackling fireplace that sent dense smoke up through the chimney. The puddle of water beneath the monster was increasing. A large chunk of ice fell away from the monster's body. Dupré jerked as the ice crashed to the floor.

Soon the ghastly face of the monster emerged into view as the ice became liquid and dripped away. All three men got a close look at the yellow skin, the long, stitched cut that had never fully healed and ran the length of the right cheek, the whitish eye sockets, the pearly teeth showing from behind the pulled back ebony lips. The flesh hardly covered the muscles and blood vessels and added to the hideousness of the face.

Reacting quickly, Winslow thrust the gas mask down upon

the monster's face. All three men breathed with relief knowing that the monster would not revive as long as it remained on his face. Winslow assured them that the mask was merely a precaution and that it was possible that it would not revive without electrical stimulation even if the mask and ice were both removed.

Winslow motioned for them to move closer, as the rest of the ice cracked and fell away from the giant form which lay before them on the floor.

Now they could view at their convenience the features of the monster not concealed by the gas mask.

Running from one side of the somewhat high forehead to the other, and above the Neanderthal brow, was a deep, red scar, sealed by small strips of metal screwed to the skull and stitches of coarse thread.

'There,' Winslow lectured, 'according to Frankenstein's personal notes, is where he opened the skull to put in the stolen brain.'

Then Winslow pointed to the stitched scar that circumvented the monster's muscular neck.

'And note where the head was attached!' he said. 'Simply marvelous, don't you think?'

Lamont and Dupré exchanged nauseous glances.

'And notice how the monster was pieced together. See how certain corresponding organs don't particularly match. Fascinating!'

Lamont pointed to the small pieces of rounded metal that protruded from each temple, gleaming in the firelight and making a contrast with the long, black hair.

'What are these?' he asked. 'Bolts?'

'Not quite,' answered Winslow. 'Those are primitive electrodes. Through these, Victor Frankenstein sent the life-giving electrical current into his creation.'

'I still think it is a horror,' said Dupré, 'but I must also admit that it is incredible. The mind boggles, as they say.'

'What is there left for you to do, now that the monster has been put to sleep with that gas?' Morris Lamont inquired.

'Well, first of all, I'll need your help again. I want to get the monster packaged up in a wooden crate, one that's sturdy enough for a journey back to Europe. I've rented an entire railroad freight car to haul it as far as I can until I can get to a ship. Then, the monster and I head for Europe. More railroad cars in Europe, then we go to Ingoldstadt where my assistant Lynn Powell will be waiting with a truck.'

'Why don't you take a plane and save some time?' asked Dupré.

'Can't risk that,' replied Winslow. 'The airlines would never let me ride in the baggage compartment in a plane with our giant friend. And I doubt the passengers would think too highly of my taking him out of the crate and propping him up in one of the seats.'

'Hmmm,' returned Dupré, 'you certainly have everything planned in advance. It must be nice to be wealthy.'

'It is,' laughed Winslow.

Within the half hour, the three men were again at work, placing the dormant bulk of the Frankenstein monster into a coffin-like wooden box. They all leaned against the recepticle, then looked at one another.

'Well, my friends,' said Pierre Dupré, extending his hand to Winslow and shaking it firmly, 'I am afraid I must be leaving you. What I would give to go with you all the way to Ingoldstadt and see your project through to the end. But I have my job to consider. And there is still time for me to have most of my vacation with my friends up at the communications post.'

'And I,' added Lamont, 'have my business here.'

'It was good knowing the both of you,' said Winslow, 'and if there is any good publicity about the monster, I'll make sure your names get credit. Believe me, I couldn't have done this alone. Who knows, someday I may just take a trip back to this white hell and say hello.'

Dupré lifted his wounded arm up slightly from its sling and attempted to wave. Winslow and Lamont watched him take his one suitcase and walk out the door.

Lamont drove Winslow to the railroad depot, bringing the box containing the Frankenstein monster along in his truck. Both of them carried rifles, in the event that the eskimos would be brave enough to make an attack at the station. But there was no further encounter. Winslow and the owner of the transport company placed the crated monster into the box car. Then the scientist climbed into the car, returned the rifle to Lamont, and watched him drive back toward his garage.

Winslow turned away from the scene of snow covered buildings as a railroad employee shut the door of the freight car. A few minutes passed, with the doctor looking at the awesome rectangular container, and the train began to chug away from the station.

For the first time in days, Winslow slept, confident that he had gotten away without the knowledge of any vengeful natives. The darkness of the box car was welcome in that land of extended daylight.

His dreams were vague snatches of the events that had taken place in the Arctic. They had no real time to develop into full fledged nightmares for he was already being awakened by the sensation that something was tugging at his body. His eyes fluttered, focusing on the reality of the freight car and he learned, to his consternation, that powerful arms were dragging him to the open doorway. A vision of the distant snows and white coated trees streaked by before he fully realized that he was no longer sleeping.

Although he was exhausted and no longer wanted to solve his problems through violent means, Winslow knew that his life and the outcome of his project depended on breaking free of the iron grasp of his captor. Whirling about, he sent his feet flying into his assailant's jaw. He saw the eskimo slam against the floor, making an impression in the sawdust. In an instant the doctor was on his feet, seeing a second native, who had been standing behind the monster's crate, snarl at him.

Putting his college football training into practice, Winslow tackled the second eskimo as he emerged from behind the box. Both men dropped to the floor. Winslow punched his apponent's face, causing him to groan and blink in bewilderment.

But the second native was already up and on Winslow's back, pulling him backwards. The scientist struggled to break free but was still weary. He could see the other assailant rise to his feet and stomp toward him with clenched fists and a flash of white teeth. Somehow Winslow managed to use the man holding him as a brace and kick the one approaching him off balance, hearing a sickening thud as his heels made impact with a human jaw. The eskimo grunted from the pain, then sank to his knees.

Startled to see his accomplice fall, the man holding Winslow carelessly relaxed his grip. The doctor spun around and proceeded to batter him with his fists.

There was a sudden gleam of metal reflecting the rays of the sun that shone into the box car through the open door. Winslow saw the other native rushing him with an ice pick, the point aimed precariously at his chest. The doctor's hand shot inside his coat pocket and removed the .38 revolver that he had purchased from Lamont. He squeezed the trigger, firing a deadly spike of flame. The man with the ice pick moaned, staggered about the box car, and tumbled outside to become part of the passing scenery.

While Winslow saw the fate of his victim, the other eskimo grasped him from behind, crushing his throat in his powerful arms. He could feel blood in his throat from the pressure exerted by the native. In another few moments he would have been dead had he not acted swiftly. Winslow's arms shot over his head, seizing his opponent around the neck. With a mighty lunge, the doctor had tossed the eskimo forward and out to join his friend.

It was a full minute later that Burt Winslow had regained enough of his breath and composure to feel even slightly comfortable. His neck still ached and he was growing tired of being choked by vengeful natives.

Looking about the box car, he saw that two other crates had been opened. At that moment he knew how the two eskimos had been smuggled into the freight car to retrieve their stolen idol. The Frankenstein monster had not been taken from him and for that he was very thankful.

After shutting the door again, Winslow stopped and let the upper portion of his body fall limp atop the crate containing the monster. His heavy eyes began to close and his thoughts drifted away from the violence that he had just endured. This time Dr Burt Winslow really slept.

In Ingoldstadt, Lynn Powell was too busy to sleep. She had been keeping herself occupied in the castle of Frankenstein while Winslow was off on his expedition in the Arctic. More of the crates, which had been ordered and paid for in advance, had arrived at the castle.

Lynn had managed to clean up much of the filth that had covered the inside of the castle like some living, crawling growth. She cast a rather proud glance about the laboratory, seeing the stone walls where cobwebs and dust had previously been. There was a pretty smile on her lips when suddenly she heard the sound of someone knocking on the door.

'Just a moment,' she said, walking gracefully out of the laboratory with long strides. She doubted that her voice could be heard on the outside of the building.

She opened the door, which creaked as though it had not been budged since the time of Victor Frankenstein himself.

A stocky man with a long, sweeping mustache stood in the doorway. His face had rosy cheeks but not the faintest trace of a smile. After bowing formally, he looked into the girl's lovely face, totally unimpressed by her beauty.

'I shall come to the point, *frauline*,' he said. 'My name is Krag and I am the Mayor of Ingoldstadt.'

'And to what do I owe this honor?' she asked courteously.

Mayor Krag coughed, clearing his throat.

'Harrrummphf! I am not here socially,' he said. 'I wish to speak with Dr Winslow.'

'Dr Winslow is not here.'

'Not here?' he replied, puzzled. 'But the lights were on in the castle. I assumed that he would be here.'

'I had the lights on,' said Lynn. 'I am Miss Powell, his secretary and assistant. Dr Winslow is still away on his trip and I have been asked by him to take care of the castle until he returns. If you doubt my word, I have a letter written by the doctor explaining who I am and that it is all right to stay here. You are familiar with his signature from the deed to the castle which he signed.'

'Er, no, no. That's quite all right. I believe you.'

The mayor cleared his throat and tried to maintain his aura of dignity. He shrugged his shoulders and looked suspiciously about the place. It was obvious to Lynn that Krag was uneasy being in the castle. He probably expected to see the Frankenstein monster come stalking out of the shadows, she thought.

'When will Dr Winslow be returning to Ingoldstadt?'

'Shortly, I trust,' she said.

'Then I will return when the doctor comes back. The station master is a friend of mine and will inform me when that happens.' As he finished speaking he took another look about the castle, never once moving from the spot where he stood.

His eyes squinted at the many boxes that had been delivered for Dr Winslow.

'I'll tell him you were here, Mayor Krag.'

'Harrummphf! Ah, yes. But I must warn you that those crates that have been delivered here have the villagers mumbling. I don't like it when they mumble like that, for such things can lead to mob rule, you know. And that is something that I cannot control. There are crates inside and outside the castle. I could not help but notice that some have come from scientific supply houses and electrical equipment manufacturers.

'To come to the point, again, Miss Powell, they fear that your Dr Winslow may be up to the old tricks of a scientist who lived in this very building almost two hundred years ago. A scientist who had a mad dream and carried it out. The people believe the old legends. What else can they think when they see all of these boxes being delivered to Castle Frankenstein?'

Lynn already knew that what they thought was very true.

'They fear,' the Mayor concluded just before turning around and walking out the door, 'that Dr Winslow is another Victor Frankenstein, and that the dreaded monster may live again!'

CHAPTER 8

Traveling Terrors

The long journey back to Central Europe proved anything but boring for Dr Burt Winslow, even without further displays of violence or interference. The doctor's attention was always occupied considering the great scientific miracle he had been planning for so long. He hardly ever left the great box containing the dormant abomination of Frankenstein. He mused that, so long had he and the crate been together that he would feel alone once they parted company. Much of his traveling time was spent in the musty cargo holds of ships or in more damp freight cars. But he preferred to endure being uncomfortable and thus always know the fate of the box.

With luck, Winslow managed to charter an old private transport plane that condensed much of the time of journeying toward Germany. Before taking off he sent Lynn Powell a wire that he would be in Ingoldstadt before much longer. While aboard a ship or train or plane, Winslow constantly re-read portions of the book *Frankenstein* and certain pages he had copied for *The Journal of Victor Frankenstein.*

Thoughts of Lynn Powell also entered Winslow's mind. Often he would put aside his notes and stop jotting calculations on paper to think of her. The world was no longer a stretch of whiteness. There were green hills and lush forests to see now. He smiled, knowing that warmer land and a wonderful person awaited him.

A creature had suddenly appeared in the mountains near

Ingoldstadt, looking more dead than alive. His countenance was that of a dried corpse, with parched lips and sinister green eyes that stared with an unearthly fire from their cavernous sockets. He sat atop a circus wagon and grinned, showing his few yellow teeth, to the man seated next to him.

Driving the two circus wagons, which were coupled like a small train, was an enormous, brutish individual, with short cropped hair and mountainous muscles that bulged as he guided the two black stallions. He huffed and snorted, as if to compete with the noises made by the horses, and liked to spit into the passing, winding trail.

Both wagons were painted in what might have once been bright colors, but now were no more than browns, darkening yellows, and blackening reds and greens. The paint had been considerably chipped or worn away by the elements, but still boasted the words:

PROFESSOR DARTANI'S ASYLUM OF HORRORS.

'You really think we'll make some money in Ingoldstadt?' inquired the brute in his gruff voice that sounded like it was mixed with the rocks in the road.

The wagons swayed on the precarious mountain trail several times before the corpse-like Professor Dartani answered.

'You have no need to worry about that, Gort,' said the professor, his wild, strawlike hair wavering in the breeze. The almost toothless mouth smiled, wrinkling even more the sunken cheeks. 'I have never failed you before.'

'But,' said Gort, looking at the Professor and then gazing back to the road, 'This town of Ingoldstadt is supposed to be such a small, hick place. I don't see how we can make money up in this neck of the woods.'

'Fool!' said Professor Dartani, the only man living who would dare insult Gort. 'This is a superstitious town we're going to. Superstitious peasants and villagers, they are. The kind that go off and drive a stake through the first corpse that shows no signs of decay. These people believe in vampires and their ilk. Idiots! One and all! They should be glad to pay to see our show and view those things which invade their dreams at night. By coming to my exhibit, they'll be able to confront their fears that go bump in the night.'

'Yeah,' said Gort, 'and we'll be able to confront their money. And do some robberies on the side. That sounds all right to me.' As he spoke, he turned his head, letting the sun shine down on a red scar that ran diagonally across his forehead.

'Ah, Gort,' cackled Professor Dartani, 'what would I do without you to drive the wagons? My old bones are weak, heh, but then it is not my arms that give me power and strength.'

The ancient man grinned, letting his mind traverse time, to the day he had first met his servant Gort. The brute had been fleeing the United States, where the authorities had been relentlessly pursuing him for crimes of murder, kidnapping, armed robbery, and arson. The Professor had found him one day hiding from local gendarmes in the Swiss Alps. Needing a servant with Gort's own strength and immorality, he took him in as a driver. Several times it was Gort's ape-like prowess that saved him from a lone policeman.

Gort guided the horses steadily along the unpaved road. A sign told them that Ingoldstadt was not a very long drive away.

When the traveling horror show rumbled into the town, Professor Dartani said, 'Stop here, Gort. We shall not have to wait long. This appears to be a main street of Ingoldstadt.'

The old man's words proved prophetic for in hardly any time at all the street was crowded with people, dressed in quaint Germanic clothing. They buzzed about the street, coming out of homes and shops and huddling about the circus wagons. One man wearing short leather pants and high woolen stockings looked with disgust upon the elderly proprietor of the show. Professor Dartani ignored him, accustomed as he was to public scorn and derision.

To one side of the wagon was the town hall. Dartani observed that a rotund man with a long mustache was watching them from a window.

Meanwhile, the townspeople gawked at the lurid PRO-FESSOR DARTANI'S ASYLUM OF HORRORS printed with lettering to simulate human blood. Beneath the lettering was a crudely painted rendition of a cloaked skeleton, manacing a well endowed, scantily dressed red haired girl with gore dripping from a meat cleaver. She was depicted as screaming, awaiting the descent of the cleaver that would inevitably be cutting into her quite large and mostly exposed breasts.

By the time Professor Dartani stood up, he was peering out over an impressive crowd of people, some of which were pushing to get right in front of the wagon. Inside of himself, the

Professor laughed as the people mumbled in an insect-like drone, and as several women of the town gasped and tried to turn away from the skeleton and its luscious victim-to-be.

The mummy-like showman raised his lean hands into the air, bringing the crowd to a silent hush. As he observed their wide-eyed faces, Dartani knew that the audience was already his to manipulate.

He picked up a megaphone in his shivering hands and placed it to his lips.

'No need to crowd,' he said through the conical amplifying device, 'there is room for all of you to hear and see.'

The group of people murmured for a few moments, then became silent again.

'I am Professor Dartani, and this is my Asylum of Horrors. Yes, horrors, the type which cause your most terrible nightmares,' he said melodramatically, his words being pronounced incredibly clearly considering his almost total lack of teeth.

Gort, unnoticed as all the townspeople were watching his master, chuckled gruffly.

'They are all here, my friends,' said Dartani. 'Werewolves, seeking out their human prey by the light of the full moon! Blood-sucking vampires, creatures subject to the laws of their bible, the *Ruthvenian*, riding the night winds with the bats and searching for your throats with their fangs!'

Most of the people in the crowd reached for their own necks as if to insure that there were no wounds or dripping blood.

'Zombies,' the Professor went on, 'walking deadmen, once alive as you and I, now wandering the Earth with no wills of their own and existing only to obey their Voodo masters! Witches and warlocks, who conjure up from hell all manners of supernatural evil!'

The man who had been spying upon them from the town hall was bolting down the street, as fast as his stocky body would permit. Gort's head turned to see the man approaching. Within seconds, he was pushing himself through the crowd. The townspeople, noticing who the man was, parted, letting him pass between two walls of human beings. He stormed by the picture of the hooded skeleton and coughed.

'Harrummphf!' he said. 'Now see here!' But his voice was unheard with Dartani shouting through the megaphone.

59

'Ghouls who feed on the corpses of your loved ones!' the pitchman went on, almost reaching a frenzy in his enthusiasm. 'And Satan himself who –'

'I say, you there!' shouted Mayor Krag, tugging at Dartani's pant leg.

Professor Dartani kicked his foot slightly, trying to rid his leg of the meddlesome intruder.

'Torture devices! The Iron Mistress, the rack, used to make people confess to crimes too heinous to mention on a public street!'

As he finished speaking, Dartani noticed that his audience was paying less attention to him and more to the roly poly man who was standing just below him. Finally the Professor put aside the megaphone and gazed with burning eyes at the man.

'And what is the matter with you?' Dartani croaked, his lips making grotesque shapes with every syllable.

Mayor Krag shivered as the ghastly visage beamed down at him. 'Here, here,' he said, 'what do you think you are doing in this street?'

'Doing? Why, I am promoting my show,' he said, proudly waving his hand to indicate the circus wagons. 'And what do you think *you* are doing?'

Dartani's eyes burned at the husky Mayor.

'Why, I am putting an end to all this nonsense. That's what I am doing!'

'You are?' asked Dartani, making his scratchy voice as gruff as possible. 'And just who do you think you are, my overweight friend?'

Krags' face flushed with most of the redness concentrated in his round cheeks.

'I am the Mayor,' he said, taking a dignified stand and placing his thumbs in the pocket of his brown vest. 'Mayor Krag. That is who I am. And I say that you cannot set up your chamber of horrors in Ingoldstadt.'

Gort was sitting up and clenching his fists. Dartani touched his shoulder and slightly shook his head.

'And why can't I?' Dartani wanted to know, now speaking without the megaphone but still throwing his voice to the people standing at the rear of the crowd.

'Our town is fed up with terror,' said Mayor Krag. 'Many

years ago, we had our own horror in Ingoldstadt. We do not plan to suffer anymore.'

The gathering of townspeople were droning. Dartani could see how uneasy they had suddenly become as if all of them were recalling some past catastrophe.

'Bah!' said the Professor, with a look of sarcasm crawling across his lined face. 'You don't actually believe in creatures of the night, do you *mein herr*?'

'What I believe or don't believe is not the issue here,' returned Krag. 'But we have had our share of horrors in this town and don't want more. There is already enough tension and fear of the dark. We don't need your vampires and ghouls and what-nots to bring us more things to give nightmares.'

'But the monsters in my show are only exhibits. Dummies designed to thrill and titilate the imagination,' Dartani protested, wrinkling his face.

'I'll not hear another word about it,' said Krag. 'The matter is closed. I am the Mayor here and I say that you pack up your werewolves and torture racks and leave Ingoldstadt, unless you would prefer setting up your exhibits in our very fine jail.'

Professor Dartani did not say a word. But his green eyes were burning, searing into the eyes of the Mayor. Krag made an effort to turn away but was caught in a glow of olive light. A psychic bond seemed to join the two men as the gathering of townspeople, the circus wagons, and even the town of Ingoldstadt seemed to blur and vanish to some other world. To Krag, the Professor was all that existed. Then Dartani himself also disappeared, leaving only his two powerful eyes floating in a sea of shapeless vibrations. A strange, unexplainable pressure suddenly seemed to crush the Mayor's brain. His body began to perspire and quiver until at last he threw his hands before his eyes and rubbed them hysterically. When he again saw his beloved Ingoldstadt, there was no sign of Dartani, his oafish assistant, or the two Asylum of Horrors wagons.

The crowd of people who had been observing the cadaverous pitchman were now huddled around Krag, looking at him in astonishment.

'What happened to me?' he asked.

'You must have been standing there for five minutes,' said

Heinrich Franz, a townsman whom the Mayor had known most of his life.

'What!' said Krag, looking at Franz incredulously. 'Five minutes? That's utterly impossible!'

Then he turned, hearing the sound of wagon wheels. He saw the two circus wagons passing under a brick archway that led outside the town. He started to hurry after the wagons but the sudden snap of a whip caused the two black horses to pull their burden faster. By the time Mayor Krag had reached the archway, the Asylum of Horrors was already merging with the verdant splendor of the forest.

CHAPTER 9

A New Frankenstein?

When the railroad train chugged into the Ingoldstadt station, and Burt Winslow emerged from the freight car, he was greeted by a number of people.

Lynn Powell was waiting at the platform in all her blonde radiance. Standing next to her were two gray clad laborers whom his assistant had hired for him. Lynn was smiling, but the workers had long, disinterested faces, looking as if they would be glad when their work was finished.

There were other people awaiting Winslow at the station. Thirty-five scowling townspeople stood at one end of the depot platform, grimacing and mumbling to one another and bearing picket signs with words hastily scrawled in English:

WE DON'T WANT ANOTHER MONSTER-MAKER!
BURT WINSLOW – LEAVE INGOLDSTADT!
DR WINSLOW – THE NEW FRANKENSTEIN!

Mayor Krag was also waiting on the platform. His face bore the look of animosity that Winslow had remembered from their meeting in his office some time ago. The American scientist tried to ignore the townspeople and their signs and looked toward the vision of beauty who was rushing toward him.

'Lynn!' he called, jumping from the box car.

Lynn Powell hurried to him, her golden hair flowing behind her. She put her arms around him and he crushed her body against his, feeling her full breasts pressing into his chest.

Winslow felt his being electrified. He had missed her when he was away. They looked into each others eyes and Winslow crushed her to him for a lingering kiss.

The noise made by the protestors was becoming louder. The scientist raised his eyes and then took his lips away from Lynn's. With his arm firmly holding the girl around the waist, Winslow boldly marched toward the townspeople.

'What's all this for?' he asked. 'Mayor Krag, is this display necessary?'

The heavyset town official cleared his throat.

'I will not welcome you back, Dr Winslow,' said Mayor Krag. 'And neither will my people. I could not stop them from greeting you at the station with their signs. They do not wish to see another Frankenstein tragedy in Ingoldstadt.'

'You think there will be another?' asked Winslow coldly.

'We have eyes!' shouted a voice from the crowd.

'The crates!' yelled another voice. 'We have seen your crates, would-be Frankenstein!'

'The crates?' asked Winslow.

'Yes,' answered the Mayor. 'All those crates that were driven up to the castle with your name on them. Crates that were labeled in such a way that we know they contained laboratory and electrical equipment.'

'So?' asked Winslow. 'Does that make me a Frankenstein? You know I'm a scientist. I have carried my experiments from the United States to Germany. I paid for that equipment and it's mine. I have broken none of your precious laws.'

'I did not accuse you of breaking the law, Dr Winslow. What bothers me and all my townspeople is *why* you have this equipment. I can think of only two reasons for bringing such demonic machines into Castle Frankenstein. Either you are creating a new living horror, for which I hope your soul is eternally damned, or else and worse, you are bringing back the original to Ingoldstadt.'

'What I plan to do with my own legally owned property is my own business, *mein herr*,' answered Winslow forcibly. 'When I break the law, then come with your pickets and your gendarmes and arrest me. Until then, stay off my back, and my property. Good day, gentlemen!'

Winslow turned his back to the townspeople. They were still mumbling over his arrogance when he took Lynn Powell by the arm and strode back toward the freight car. By the time the scientist looked back at the crowd, they were dispersing, with Krag not knowing what to do next. Finally, the Mayor joined them, leaving Winslow, Lynn, and the two hired workers at the station.

'Can we hurry this up, Herr Winslow?' asked one of the men.

'Sure,' said the doctor. 'Come on.'

The two laborers walked to the box car and Winslow pointed to the ominous appearing wooden crate within. Upon his instruction, they carried the heavy box into a panel truck which was parked alongside the station. Their eyes were wide as they thought of the contents of that receptacle. Winslow mused that they would probably be running through the streets of the town if they knew that their suspicions concerning the crate were entirely correct.

As Winslow and Lynn climbed into the back of the truck where the crate had been placed, they noticed a few of the residents of the town peering at them from behind a wall of the station.

One of the men crossed himself and said with heavy breath, 'The Frankenstein curse is back upon us again. May Almighty God in heaven protect us, for after this day, no one will be safe in their beds.'

'It looks just like a large coffin,' said a husky woman wearing a full skirt that reached way below her knees. 'A coffin big enough for a giant.'

'Or for the monster,' moaned the man standing beside her.

But soon there was no hearing the townspeople who gathered once more in the trail of exhaust fumes made by the departing truck. The vehicle sped out of the town and up the hilly road to Castle Frankenstein.

The dark clouds were assuming grotesque shapes in the sky over Castle Frankenstein when the truck stopped before the drawbridge of the ancient structure. The monster had come back to its place of birth, thought Winslow, as the two hired men removed the crate from the truck. Winslow jumped from the truck, and helped Lynn to the ground.

Winslow instructed the men to bring the crate over the drawbridge and inside the castle, making certain that they were careful with it. They carried the box as if it were a baby and set it down just outside the laboratory, which was barred from their view by a closed oak door. Winslow paid them generously for their work and hastened them on their way. With the panel truck driving back to the town, the scientist creaked shut the heavy front door, the slamming sound echoing through the bare walled castle. Then he locked the door.

'Back at last!' he exclaimed.

Lynn smiled affectionately and approached him, hoping that the scientist would again take her in his arms. Instead, he turned toward the crate and beamed.

'I've got it!' he exclaimed triumphanty. 'In this crate! The actual body of the Frankenstein monster.'

After a minor disappointment, Lynn tried to get equally enthralled by Winslow's conquest. She too had waited so long to see it. And even though she hardly shared the doctor's fanatical enthusiasm over the gruesome discovery, she was genuinely interested.

'You are going to show it to me, aren't you?' she asked, feigning a pout.

'Oh, I'm sorry,' he replied. 'Certainly, certainly. I suppose I got carried away. Come on, Lynn. I'll show you the monster. But you'd better take a deep breath, first. The brute isn't a pretty sight.'

'I think I can take it,' she laughed. 'I'm a big girl now.'

'That, even a mad scientist like I can see,' he said, smiling, making Lynn's cheeks turn red.

Winslow produced a crowbar from a toolkit in the laboratory, then hastily pried off the lid of the crate. Eagerly he pushed aside the wooden lid, hinged by nails that squeaked as they bent.

'Okay, if you think you can stand it, take a look,' he said.

The blonde girl cautiously approached the open crate and looked, her blue eyes large, to behold its grisly contents. Even though the gas mask was still attached to the monster's face, there was enough yellow flesh, red scars, and matted black hair showing to make her ill. Winslow sensed that she was about to faint and rushed to her, bracing her body with his strong arms.

'Try not to look at it as a monster,' Winslow instructed her. 'Remember that, despite the way he looks, this being was created as a man by another man, by Victor Frankenstein with his own two hands. Try to look at it as a miracle of science!'

Lynn finally snapped out of what almost appeared to be a trance. She looked away from the giant in tattered clothes and into Winslow's face.

'I'm sorry,' she apologized. 'I had no idea it would look that bad.'

'Nobody can look at the monster without feeling queasy, Lynn. Nobody human, anyway. But now you and I have to become dedicated scientists. There is work to be done and we're not going to rely on the townspeople for help.'

Without another word, Burt Winslow grasped the crowbar firmly and rushed to where the other crates had been placed. He tore into the wooden container and exposed a section of a generator.

'Victor Frankenstein used lightning in his experiment,' said Winslow, cutting away the rest of the crate to show the entire generator. 'That was fine for his early science. But I have forsaken the lightning for my own, more practical and predictable methods. I'm in no position to sit around waiting for an electrical storm. That's why I have all of this new equipment, including portable generators.'

Frantically, Winslow continued to open the crates of electrical apparatus. Soon Lynn had taken another crowbar and was yanking away the pieces of wood to find the gauges, glassware, and varied machinery. As she helped unpack the equipment, Lynn's face revealed her curiosity.

'Tell me, Burt,' she said. 'Just why are you doing this? Just why would anyone want to revive that ugly monster?'

Winslow paused for a moment, setting aside a coil of wire, and gazed at a barren, stone wall.

'Why?' he said somberly. 'I never really thought of that. I suppose just for the sheer scientific marvel of it. It's like climbing a mountain that has never been climbed before, Lynn. And let's face it. Except for Frankenstein himself, no one has ever done this experiment.'

CHAPTER 10

To Walk Again

Night had swallowed the town of Ingoldstadt. But this was no ordinary night. It was a night electrified by fear. Numerous buildings in the town were illuminated by flickering lights that appeared as yellow eyes, giving life to homes and shops. Inside the Red Galley Inn, patrons were chatting about the awesome, coffin shaped box that had been sent to Castle Frankenstein. The air of the inn was a cloud of cigarette, cigar, and pipe smoke that had settled over the heads of the customers.

Heinrich Franz took a long draught from his beer stein, then, with a bit of foam still on his lips, set the mug on the table. He wiped the foam from his mouth and stared at the two men who were seated at the table with him.

'I don't like it,' said Heinrich Franz to Braun and Ulrich. 'I don't like it one bit. It is too much like the old days. My father and grandfather and his father all passed along the story of Frankenstein and the monster made from corpses.'

The other men seated at the table grunted in agreement, then continued drinking their beer, all the while listening attentively to Franz.

'Now it looks like the devil's experiment of Frankenstein is going to happen again,' he said. 'Once again the monster will prowl our streets, searching for someone to rip apart with its gigantic hands.'

One of the two men finished off his beer and waved the empty mug before Franz' eyes.

'We had better all keep our eyes open,' said Braun.

'More than that, *mein herr*,' returned Franz. 'We'd best keep our eyes peeled on Castle Frankenstein. And at the first sign of trouble, we'll deal with this Dr Winslow and his wench the way our ancestors would have done.'

The waiter approached the table and Heinrich Franz ordered another round of beer for himself and his friends. Then he leaned back in his wooden chair and smiled.

A crackling campfire was the only illumination in the clearing of the dense woods. The trees cast elongated, wavering shadows across the camp, wriggling along the sides of the circus wagons. The aroma of beans cooking over the fire drifted to the nostrils of the pair of magnificent stallions, who waited patiently, tied to a tree.

Gort turned a spoon in the bubbling cauldron of beans and whiffed the aroma.

Professor Dartani sat atop a rock, staring out into the blackness of the forest. His back was to the campfire and he seemed hardly interested in the food. Something else had taken possession of his mind and had apparently removed his spirit from the campsite.

Gort looked up at his master and said, 'Anything the matter? You can't afford to lose any weight, you know. Why not join me in some beans? They're good. I cooked them myself.'

But Professor Dartani did not budge. Gort looked in the direction that the Professor's green eyes stared into the darkness but saw only the shadowy forms of great trees and the black silhouette of a castle.

'I said anything the matter?' Gort said, speaking louder.

Like one of the dummies from his own Asylum of Horrors, Professor Dartani slowly turned toward his driver. His mummy-like countenance bore a look of sheer hatred that made even the brute criminal uncomfortable.

'I have been thinking of,' he began with contempt, 'Krag.'

'Mayor Krag?'

Dartani nodded. 'The impudent fool! The way he thought he could tell me where I could or could not show my exhibits! But the overstuffed fool shall pay for what he has done.'

A sadistic grin moved Gort's lips. He rubbed his hands together in anticipation of performing some act of cruelty.

'Do you want me to sneak back into town,' he said to the

69

Professor, 'and slit his throat? Or I can . . . '

'Not just yet,' said Dartani, his bones creaking as he slowly made his way off the rock. 'Not just yet.'

'Well, when?' asked Gort, smiling hideously, his teeth flashing in the fire glow, at the thought of being able to take another human life. 'It has been a long time since I've had any pleasure.'

'I must plan first,' answered Professor Dartani. 'If you were to creep into town and kill our Mayor Krag, we would probably be the first persons to be suspected for the murder. And these old wagons could never escape the horses of the gendarmes. No, Gort, we must wait. Wait and plan. Plan something very special for our dear Mayor Krag for his insults.'

'Couldn't we kill him and take the body with us?'

Dartani shook his head. 'Are you that stupid not to see that we would be suspected even if the Mayor were only missing? I know how anxious you are to get those powerful hands of yours working again. I know how torturous it can be to be idle, especially for someone with such special needs and talents as yourself. But be patient and you shall soon have your fun.'

The brute walked to the campfire and spooned out two plates of hot beans. He handed one to the Professor and began to devour his own portion.

'But for the present,' said the Professor, again gazing out toward the black woods and castle, 'we wait.'

The laboratory that had been set up in Castle Frankenstein hardly resembled the ruins first discovered by Winslow when he purchased the old building. The rusted, archaic equipment of Victor Frankenstein had been replaced by Winslow with the best new equipment that any fortune could buy. The expensive generator, connected to the river-driven paddle wheel outside the castle, occupied one corner of the room. Pieces of impossible looking electrical apparatus filled almost every cranny of the laboratory, with great terminals and coils and rheostats just waiting to be sparked into operation.

In the center of the laboratory was the replacement for Victor Frankenstein's wooden table. Winslow had erected a metal platform, some ten feet in length, equipped with five buckle-down leather straps and tilted to a forty-five degree angle with the floor. There was a metal footrest at the base of the platform.

Reclining on the platform, motionless and silent, was the awesome hulk of the Frankenstein monster. The assemblage of transplanted organs was securely bound to the platform by leather straps with the raised, black boots of the monster atop the footrest. The eyes, set in their white sockets, were closed. The gas mask had been removed and the creature's corpse-like face was completely exposed for view. Thus far the monster did not come out of his state of dormancy, but Winslow was glad that he had taken the precaution of the gas mask. Now if the monster revived premature to the final experiment it would hardly matter. The scientist doubted even the giant could snap those bonds.

'I still think it's ghastly,' said Lynn Powell, standing before the Frankenstein monster in her short, white nurse's uniform that revealed her gorgeous legs. 'I'll be glad when you've finished this experiment and proven whatever it is you hope to prove. Then maybe we can live like normal human beings and stop thinking of laboratories and dead bodies.'

'It won't be long now, Lynn,' he said, making some last minute adjustments on one of the electrical devices. 'I'm glad the monster hasn't revived without the benefit of this apparatus. There's no telling what damage there might have been to its tissues if he returned to life after being frozen for almost two centuries. Now we'll bring it back the right way.'

Lynn completed her own adjustments of the equipment as Winslow grasped two lengths of cable, each terminating in a socket-like device. Taking the cables, which had already been connected to the laboratory machinery, the scientist climbed a ladder to the top of the metal platform and connected each snaky length to the two electrodes imbedded in the temples of the Frankenstein monster.

'We'll send the life-giving power to him through these cables,' said Winslow, looking back at his assistant. Lynn was bending over the control panel, checking out the switches and dials, and looking fetching in the tight fitting uniform. For a short while Winslow managed to smile, considering the fact that he was working with such a vision and not with any ugly and deformed assistant named Igor.

He re-checked the electrode connections, then climbed down

from the platform and stood beside Lynn. They both gazed up at the monstrous form on the platform.

'You know,' he said with a grin, 'it doesn't look so bad with the new black pants and coat and that black turtle neck sweater we got him. Those old clothes it had on were nothing but tattered rags.'

'It's still hideous,' she said, 'the way those long arms stick out of the sleeves, and with all those scars and stitches and everything.'

'It may be hideous, but it was created to be a man. Only when it was scoffed by the world of normally born human beings, and when it was rejected by its own creator, did it become a "monster". I suppose I would too if I were such a tormented creature. And think, Lynn,' he raved, hurrying to the monster and touching the enormous chest with his hands, 'we are about to prove that man can create man!'

'I still don't like looking at it,' she said. 'I wonder if I'll ever get used to it.'

'Perhaps,' said Winslow. 'But now we must not worry about how the monster looks. We are here to make it walk again.'

Recalling all that he had mentally photographed of the Frankenstein journal, plus his own calculations for incorporating Frankenstein's techniques with his own, Winslow began to work on bringing the monster back to the world of living men. First, he took the serum which he had prepared according to Frankenstein's notes and injected the life-giving substance into the monster's sinewy yellow arm.

Then he picked two pairs of dark lensed goggles up from a table, donned one pair and gave the other pair to Lynn. She still looked bewitching even with the goggles covering her blue eyes. He took her hand and led her to the control panel, over which they could see the monster.

Four hands rested on dials and switches. Two hearts were pounding with almost machine-gun rapidity.

'Are you ready?' asked Winslow. His fingers were tense around the plastic dials.

'Yes,' answered Lynn. 'Let's start.'

'All right, here we go!'

Taking a deep breath, Winslow twisted the first dial. Then he turned the second one and began to flick the switches on the control panel. Lynn was also working her controls according to the way the two of them had rehearsed the experiment. Everything would have to go according to Winslow's schedule.

As Winslow and Lynn Powell worked the controls, the laboratory became alive with electrical splendor. Lights of different colors began to flash. The dark goggles shielded their eyes from the ever increasing display of throbbing, incandescent power. Great jagged arcs of electricity jumped from one terminal to the next. The laboratory was buzzing, erupting with the forces of science, with the stench of ozone permeating the air.

On the platform, the monster's composite body remained still. The eyelids stayed closed.

Winslow increased the power until his ears ached from the noises exploding from the machinery. Crackling blue-white sparks leapt unbelievable lengths about the terminals. Ribbons of electricity shot about the smoking electrodes while the long cables continued pouring the pseudo forces of life into the monster's body. Wheels spun, shooting off sparks. Noises crashed above other noises. Gauges pumped their indicators back and forth as if fighting to burst through the glass which confined them.

All the while, Winslow and Lynn watched the monster with their hands constantly guiding the controls. The doctor leaned forward on the control board. His heart nearly leapt from his chest. He knew that it was not his imagination. He knew that he saw the monster's face twitch.

The laboratory was now a pandemonium of electricity.

The monster's face jerked sharply. The massive body moved in a great convulsion.

Winslow jumped aside of the control panel for a better look. He saw the monster's black lips part to drink in the electrically charged air. A deafening *boom!* reverberated throughout the chamber and the monster's dull, sulphurous eyes opened. The disfigured head turned on the platform and two yellow orbs gazed at the two people in white.

Instantly, Winslow became elated, almost insane with the sense of power.

'It's alive!' Winslow reared, hugging Lynn tightly. 'Do you realize what we've done? The Frankenstein monster is *alive!*'

Then he released her to marvel at the monster. Lynn shrugged, not from the ugly features of the living horror on the platform, but from Winslow himself. Never before had she seen such a wild look in the scientist's eyes.

Residents of Ingoldstadt heard the noises emitting from the open windows of Castle Frankenstein. The brightly illuminated windows of the castle glowered against the night sky and could be seen even as far away as the town. Soon much of the town's population was standing in the street, making the sign of the cross as they looked toward the flickering black shape on the hill.

'There, you see!' shouted one of the townspeople. 'See what is happening at Castle Frankenstein.'

Mayor Krag was running out to the street in his bathrobe to see the townspeople standing, shouting, raising their fists high above their heads.

'The lights in the castle!' yelled another man. 'My great-grandfather told me stories of what happened when the lights of Castle Frankenstein flashed in the night. The monster from hell came to life!'

'Now we know it is no legend! We no longer have any doubts! Our ancestors did not lie to us!'

'Dr Winslow!' shouted a woman. 'He's as bad as Frankenstein himself! Let's get him and put an end to him!'

Before the crowd had a chance to move, Krag had whipped out his revolver and fired it several times into the sky. The sudden blasts of yellow fire brought the crowd to a standstill. All heads turned to the mayor.

'Wait,' warned Mayor Krag. 'Winslow has still broken no laws. He said that he would be experimenting in the castle.'

The murmurs increased.

'But we saw the crate he took from the train,' said another man.

'Yes,' said Krag, 'a crate that could have contained anything.'

'Like the monster!' The word *monster* brought the crowd out of their murmuring and back to shouting.

Krag fired again into the air.

'All of you, listen to me. That crate probably contained laboratory equipment and nothing more.'

'Bah! You drove that horror show out of Ingoldstadt. What stops you from doing the same with this Winslow?'

'Because,' said Krag, 'Winslow has not broken any laws nor shown us any monster. But if the monster does walk again, I'll personally deal with him, with the police at my side. As for now we can't invade a man's property just because of some flashing lights. All of you, go back home to bed. Don't invent demons that are not there. The police have already been ordered to patrol the streets and stop any mob action that may be taking place. Go home!'

The townspeople were grumbling as they returned to their homes and places of business. But three of them had remained in the shadows and were already making their way toward Castle Frankenstein. The leader of the small group said to his partners as they hid behind a clump of bushes less than a hundred yards away from the castle drawbridge, 'There it is. If the Frankenstein monster is about this night, the three of us'll know about it.'

'B-but what if the monster sees us, Heinrich?' asked the man to his right.

'Don't be a coward, Ulrich,' said Heinrich Franz with confidence. 'It will never see us in this underbrush. No, *mein herr*, I will be the first to report the monster. Then we'll all be important in Ingoldstadt. Perhaps I will be the next mayor and you will be in my employ.'

'Now that it's alive again, it looks worse than ever,' said Lynn Powell, looking with horror upon the strapped down figure of the monster.

The monster's head turned, its heavy eyelids blinking in bewilderment from beneath the sloping brow. The straight lips parted and the monster screamed such a scream that both Lynn and Winslow reacted with antipathy.

'Oh, Burt,' said Lynn, turning away and burying her face in her hands, 'he must be in terrible pain. Stop the experiment. Please.'

'I can't stop it now, Lynn. Switching off the machines now would be disastrous for the monster. It would always be in pain.'

The monster was looking about, straining to free himself from the restraining straps. Then, surprisingly, its head lay still against the platform. The electrodes continued to spark and

75

sizzle while the laboratory never relented in its display of electrical power.

But the Frankenstein creature did not scream again. There was something happening within its transplanted brain. For a while it had been confused after being so long in its icy prison. Now its thoughts were becoming organized. Memories of the past may have been vague, but the beast could discern that the experiment that had given its life so long ago was being recreated but on a grander scale. The monster recalled the way he had been born into a world of misunderstanding, hating men who drove it away and tried to snatch away the life to which it so tenaciously held. There was peace with the death of the frozen wastes but now there was the new horror of returning to its previous, unwanted existence.

Lynn ran behind the control panel while Winslow, not understanding, increased the power.

The monster snarled and looked toward the man working the controls, seeing in him the face of his creator. The yellow hands formed mammoth fists. The muscles of the mismatching arms flexed like twisted steel. Two electrically charged arms pushed up on the leather straps and ripped through them with ease.

Winslow gasped as he saw the Frankenstein monster tear off the thick strap that held its chest to the platform, then it yanked the coils from the electrodes on its head and leant over to remove the straps restraining the legs. Sparks shot from the two cables that wriggled across the floor until Lynn threw the switches that cut off the power. Lights made attempts to flicker. The humming sounds dwindled to silence. And the once great arcs of electricity fizzled out. The laboratory was dead.

But the monster lived!

And was free!

The Frankenstein monster awkwardly stepped down from the platform, its heavy boots thudding against the stone floor. It stretched its long arms and smiled with a grim satisfaction, realizing that its superhuman strength had been restored along with its unnatural life.

Then the monster's yellow eyes focused on Winslow. The black lips formed a cold sneer as if to say that although it did not want its life restored, now it would treasure that life and never release it.

For the first time in nearly two hundred years, the monster

of Frankenstein stiffly walked toward Winslow.

The scientist was totally baffled as to how to handle the situation. He had thought the monster would have been glad to return to the world of the living. And yet the grim expression on that grisly face told him otherwise.

With reluctance, Winslow backed away from the monster, with the giant following him with slow yet enormous strides.

'Wait,' said Winslow, 'you don't understand. I brought you back to life. This is a different world than the one in which you were created. I will not be like Frankenstein. I'll help you, take care of you. Don't you understand? Can't you speak to me? You once had the power of speech.'

The monster only growled. It was nearing Winslow with every giant step and its lengthy, powerful fingers were stretched and reaching for the youthful scientist.

Winslow stepped back until he bumped hard against the machinery that had been propped against the wall. The monster was upon him within a few additional steps. The doctor's face perspired as he looked up into the ugly face towering two feet above him. There was no denying that he was trapped by the creature and about to be slaughtered. His own death no longer mattered to him. But the thought of Lynn's fate and that of the people of Ingoldstadt weighed heavily upon his conscience.

'Lynn!' he pleaded as the monster's lips showed a terrible grin. 'Get out of here!'

But Lynn Powell was petrified with fright. At last she managed to scream as the monster's mighty right hand locked like a fleshy vise around Winslow's neck. Winslow's eyes bulged from their sockets and a gag caught within his throat as the monster squeezed.

CHAPTER 11

When Menaces Meet

Two men gaped with wonder at the distant gothic structure that had, just moments before, been alive with strange noises and stranger lights.

Professor Dartani marveled at the structure and spoke to the muscular figure standing to his right.

'You know,' he said, 'I have done much reading about this part of Europe. It is said that on the outskirts of Ingoldstadt exists an ancient castle. And in that castle, according to the legends, a scientist named Frankenstein created a living monster.'

'Frankenstein?' said Gort, scratching his head. 'But I thought . . . '

'I know. You thought it was only a story. But remember what Mayor Krag said about Ingoldstadt having its own horrors. I didn't make the association before, but this may very well be what he meant.'

'Frankenstein's castle,' said Gort with awe.

'Hmmm. You know, Gort, I never made the association because I never believed in the legend. But judging from the activity that seems to have been going on in the castle tonight, I don't know.'

Dartani's green eyes seemed to take on a glow in the firelight.

'Perhaps some of the creatures in my Asylum of Horrors can be more than just dummies. Something has obviously been happening here. Something that has stopped.'

'So what does that mean for us?' asked Gort, trying to reason out his master's thinking. 'What do you think?'

'At the moment I do not think anything,' said the horror show proprietor. 'But perhaps . . . soon I shall know.'

Again Lynn Powell screamed.

But Winslow could not even gasp with the monster's grip forcing the life out of his body. Winslow could feel the fingers pressing his neck and knew that they would soon meet, crushing through his bones with hardly any effort.

The yellow orbs of the monster's eyes stared into Winslow's face, delighting in his helplessness, smiling as he saw the scientist's tongue hang limply from his mouth. The black lips pulled back to reveal the white, uneven teeth.

The scientist knew that the monster could destroy him without the slightest effort. But for some inexplicable reason the monster had not yet killed him. The eyes of the giant blinked and, to Winslow's bewilderment, the powerful fingers suddenly relaxed and released him. The doctor stumbled back against the machinery, grasping his aching throat. Then with a clumsy turn, the monster lumbered away from the man who had given it new life.

Cautiously, Lynn emerged from behind the control board. As the monster passed her she thought to see its yellow orbs meet hers. But all that mattered to her was Winslow; and all that apparently mattered to the monster was the freedom of the outdoors.

As Lynn rushed to Winslow and caressed his throat, the scientist perceived the monster lumbering toward the main door of the castle. He watched as the creature of Frankenstein grasped the handle of the ancient door, yanked with the full force of its mighty arms, and pulled it open despite the twentieth century lock.

Then the monster stalked into the night, its black clothing merging with the darkness.

Winslow reacted, making a lunge for the door and still feeling the pain in his neck.

'No,' said Lynn, grabbing and embracing him. 'You're not going out into that darkness.'

Burt shook his head as if to clear his mind, then pulled Lynn to him.

'Oh, Burt,' she said, letting her tears dampen Winslow's

surgical smock, 'what have we done?'

'You mean, what have *I* done,' he corrected her. 'It was I who unleashed that horror upon the countryside.' He stepped aside and lowered his head, standing next to the platform from which the monster had broken loose. 'I had to do something spectacular, something that would really impress the scientific world. Well, I succeeded. And look what happened.'

Winslow walked to the door of the castle and looked out to the darkness. Lynn followed him to the door. Holding hands firmly, they entered the castle and shut the door.

The young scientist wondered what he would do next.

Heinrich Franz and his accomplices concealed themselves in the woods near Castle Frankenstein, totally out of view of the main door.

'Listen,' Heinrich Franz whispered to Ulrich and Braun. 'Do you hear that?'

Ulrich and Braun listened intently and heard the steady thump, thump, thump of heavy footsteps crushing foliage. The steps were becoming louder and they knew that someone was approaching.

'Now that the lights have stopped,' said Braun, 'whoever it is that's coming might be from the castle. If it's who I think it is, then I'm going back to town.' Automatically, he started in the direction of Ingoldstadt.

But Franz's strong hand clamped upon his shoulder, bringing him to a stop. He raised a long rifle into the moonlight, the barrel shining blue.

'No one's running just yet,' said Franz. 'We've got rifles. We're going to see this through. Now stay close together.'

Standing together with ready weapons, the three men heard the footsteps grow louder. Suddenly the bushes before them rustled and a giant, shadowy form stepped into view. The three men gasped as they beheld the sickening face of the brute, a hideous scowl on its face.

'The monster!' gasped Braun. 'The Frankenstein monster!'

'Alive!' exclaimed Franz. 'You see, I was right! Now ready with those rifles, men!'

Ulrich was the first to take aim. But although he had been entrapped in ice for so long, the monster recalled the sight of a gun, a puny weapon for so formidable a creature, yet one that could inflict pain. Before Ulrich could squeeze the trigger, fingers of living steel had snatched the weapon from his hands. Franz and Braun stood petrified. Ulrich gasped and the monster snarled at the human being who had tried to cause him pain. He tried to flee from the horror but was already in the grip of the monster. Without delay, the creature had swung Ulrich around by his feet and dashed his brains across a nearby tree trunk.

The other men reacted to the horror.

Braun had already raised his rifle to enact vengeance upon the beast for the slaying of his friend. But his weapon was also caught in the clutches of the monster and snapped in half by those Herculean hands.

Heinrich Franz was already blending with the shadows of the forest when he saw his screaming comrade picked up in the monster's hands, raised into the air, and snapped over its knee. He would remember the sickening crack of Braun's spine for the rest of his days.

Then the monster turned to kill the third man, but Franz had already vanished in the darkness. Without feeling, the beast stomped past the mangled corpses and then proceeded, without destination, among the tall trees.

Professor Dartani was certain that he heard the sounds of a struggle from somewhere in the woods. His mind was still occupied by thoughts of Mayor Krag and the lights which he had seen at Castle Frankenstein. Suddenly he tensed, hearing the sounds of approaching footsteps.

'Gort,' he whispered, 'follow me.'

The two of them hid in the bushes, while the mammoth figure of the Frankenstein monster came into view. The campfire was still burning. Its light made the yellow hues of the monster's face and hands appear even more unearthly. Carefully avoiding the flames, the monster continued on its way until summoned by a shrill voice from behind.

'Wait!' shrieked Professor Dartani as he moved from the bushes.

Gort stood up with caution, expecting to see his scrawny master broken in half by the monster.

The monster turned to see what this latest man would do to cause it misery. It expected to find this adversary like the others, cowering in terror over its awesome appearance. Surprisingly, however, the little man did not fear the giant. Instead, he grinned, showing the few yellow teeth he had in his shriveled mouth, and addressed the monster with arrogance.

'You are the Frankenstein monster, I presume,' he said. 'Splendid. I have been waiting for you.'

'Frankenstein!' rasped Gort.

The monster's brain was confused as to the strange behavior of the man. One thing the creature knew, however, was that the man who addressed him was also wretched in appearance.

'I will not hurt you,' continued Dartani, 'and you will not hurt me. Am I correct?'

Dartani's green eyes blazed with mesmeric intensity. The monster's yellow orbs revolved curiously in their sockets. For a while they gaped at one another as if in some weird pyschic battle of wits.

'And you have come from the castle?'

The monster nodded, then pointed in the direction of the castle. The black lips parted but its attempts at speaking resulted only in unintelligible gasps.

'You cannot speak?' asked Dartani with mock concern. 'That is tragic, isn't it? But you understand me. That is good. Tell me, do you know what the word *friend* means? Friend?'

The monster nodded, the lengthy black hair flopping about its large shoulders.

'Well, that is what I am,' continued the Professor. 'I am your friend. *Your friend.* And no one needs to tell me that a creature like you can use a friend.'

Dartani's brow furled and his eyes seemed to glow with new brightness. He extended both of his hands to the giant.

'Here,' he said. 'Take my hands.'

The monster responded to Dartani's suggestion and held the Professor's hands. It was careful not to squeeze them too tightly. There was the hint of a smile on the creature's face.

'Good, my friend. Now notice my eyes. Stare into them and try to lose yourself as if being drowned in a green sea.'

The eyes of the monster were already being drawn into those of Professor Dartani. Its brain was newly awakened and highly susceptible to suggestion. The world into which it had been reborn was throbbing and dissolving away, leaving nothing save the soothing words and the scathing eyes of Professor Dartani.

Gort, dumbfounded, approached Professor Dartani and saw

him wave his hand before the entranced face of the demon.

'You did it,' he said.

'Quiet, fool, until I am certain.'

The monster stood before them like some ghastly lifeless figure from the Professor's horror show.

'You will obey only my commands,' said Dartani in his most forceful voice. 'Do you understand?'

The monster's head nodded up and down.

'You did it just like you said,' Gort observed. He stared up into the monster's face. 'And though it's hard to believe, this monster is for real!'

Professor Dartani turned to Gort, grinning fiendishly.

'Remember when I said that we would kill Mayor Krag but not until we had something special in mind?' asked the Professor.'

'I remember.'

'Well, now there is no longer any need to wait. We have something more special than even I had dared dream of. We have the Frankenstein monster subject entirely to my will.'

Gort again looked at the monster, who stood like a grim sentinel awaiting his orders.

CHAPTER 12

Horror Stalks the Streets

Burt Winslow was seated before a wooden table in the laboratory, his fingers playing with the pair of goggles that he had used in the experiment. His other hand wandered through his thick brown hair, mussing it.

Behind him, Lynn Powell stood and rested a gentle hand upon his shoulder. He hardly seemed to notice her.

'If I could only have made it understand,' said Winslow in a depressed voice. 'Understand that I was giving it new life.'

'Maybe it did understand,' she returned, seeing Winslow look up at her. 'Maybe that's why it came after you. Maybe it didn't want to be brought back as a misfit in an alien world.'

'Then why didn't it kill me?'

'That might have been too fast, too easy, Burt. I think the monster figured that to let you live you would suffer for what you had done. You know, experience guilt for whatever crimes it might perpetrate in this world.'

'God help me,' Winslow moaned, looking away from Lynn and letting his vision drift across the gleaming, silent electrical apparatus. 'If only I could have spoken to it. But it appears as if the many years in the ice have damaged the vocal cords. Everyone around here tried to warn me. Even you did, Lynn. But I was too stubborn, too stupid and self-centered to listen. I thought I was performing a revolutionary experiment and proving something to the world. What I did prove was that a mad scientist does not have to be an old man with frizzy hair and a dwarf assistant. Oh, Lynn, I've recreated Frankenstein's greatest mistake in all its terrible splendor.'

Then he looked upon the girl; not really at her, but as if she were some object to hide away in a secret closet.

'Lynn, you must leave Ingoldstadt immediately.'

'Leave?'

'Yes, before another minute passes, you must be at the railroad station. Take the Volkswagon I bought and speed there as fast as you can.'

'But why?' she asked.

'It's not only the monster that makes me fear for you,' he explained, standing up and holding her arms tightly. 'It's the villagers. They were on the verge of becoming a mob back at the railroad depot. Think what will happen now. Sooner or later the monster will show its ugly face to one of the townspeople. There'll be mass hysteria. And we'll be the ones they'll be after. Lynn, you've got to do this for me. You've got to get away from here!'

She shook her head.

'Nothing you say or do will drag me away from you, Burt. I'm staying until this whole mess is straightened out – somehow.'

One side of Winslow's mouth curled up into a smile.

'I wanted to hear you say that, but was afraid to.'

'I'm still the best assistant you ever had, Burt. And I intend to remain your best assistant.'

'You're more than an assistant,' he said. Then he took her in his arms and kissed her. For a minute the Frankenstein monster managed to be barricaded from his thoughts. But when the two people parted, its ghastly countenance was again haunting Winslow's mind.

'You realize it is up to me,' said the scientist, 'to track down the monster and destroy it.'

'Destroy it?' she replied, puzzled. 'But you yourself said that the monster was immortal and couldn't be killed.'

'I said it could not really die by ordinary means. But I am not thinking of ordinary means.'

Winslow searched through some surgical implements scattered upon the white cloth covering one of the tables in the laboratory. He fished out a scalpel and raised it to his eyes.

'This is my weapon. Remember how Victor Frankenstein assembled his monster,' Winslow said, turning toward Lynn, still holding the scalpel. 'Organ by organ, bit by bit. Now if I could somehow capture the monster before it does too much harm, drug him, and bring him back to the laboratory, I could reverse Frankenstein's procedure and rid the world of the horror I set loose upon it.'

'Reverse the procedure?' asked Lynn. She winced as if considering something which made her feel ill. 'You can't mean . . .'

'Yes,' said Winslow, sqeezing the scalpel until it slid with the perspiration of his hand, 'the only way to really destroy Frankenstein's monster is to dissect it.'

Mayor Krag tossed over in his comfortable bed a third time, hoping that the pounding at his door was in his dream. Anything would have been welcome in that nightmare where he saw the awesome countenance of the Frankenstein demon snarling at him through a sea of whirling blood. Krag's eyelids fluttered as the knocking persisted. He rubbed the dried particles of sleep from his eyes and sat up in the bed.

With a look of dissatisfaction, Krag turned his head in the direction of the rhythmic *thump, thump, thump.*

'Go away,' the Mayor grumbled. 'Don't you know what time it is?'

But the plea was not heeded and the knocking became even louder. At last, Mayor Krag coughed and exclaimed, 'All right, all right. I'm coming. You don't have to shake the house apart with your damned knocking.'

Still feeling the effects of slumber, Mayor Krag stood upon his tired feet and wrapped a robe about his rounded figure, then slid into his slippers.

'Who in his fool mind would be out in the middle of the night?' he moaned, shuffling his way to the door. 'I'm coming. Now stop knocking, will you?'

Mayor Krag quickly unlocked and opened the door, eager to see who he could have arrested for disturbing his sleep. Standing outside the door was his friend Heinrich Franz. But this was not the same, courageous and even foolhardy Franz that he had known his entire life. There was a look about his face that distorted his features. His eyes were wild and red and there were tears streaking his face.

'Heinrich!' asked Ingoldstadt's highest official. 'What's happened to you. You look like you've seen a ghost.'

'Worse than a ghost, Krag,' said Franz, breathing heavily. 'It's alive and I saw it! Alive!'

'What? Do you mean . . . ?'

'Krag, I saw it. The monster! With my own eyes I saw it! The demon killed Braun and Ulrich as if they were ants. Oh, it was horrible.'

Franz covered his eyes and sobbed, as he recalled the splashing of blood and the breaking of bones.

'I . . . managed to escape,' he said, 'before the monster could get to me. Oh, Krag, Krag, we've got to organize the townspeople. Hunt down that killer! Destroy it! Burn it to ashes! Before it kills anyone else!'

The condition of Heinrich Franz informed Krag that he was speaking the truth and was not influenced by the stench of beer that issued from his mouth.

'I'll call the police,' said the Mayor. 'We'll comb the countryside for this monster. Where did you see it?'

'In the woods. The monster was walking away from Castle Frankenstein.'

'Go back home, Heinrich. You'll be no good to us until you calm down. You've been through a lot. Then when you're back to your senses, you may join us in our search.'

'Y-yes,' said Franz, shivering. 'Perhaps you are right.'

Heinrich Franz left and the Mayor bolted the door after him. He watched him depart from the window, and saw how he avoided every shadow of the street.

Mayor Krag reached for the telephone and began to dial the number of the police station. But before he could finish, there was another pounding, this time more forceful than Franz's and coming from the back door. He put down the receiver.

Perhaps someone else has news of the monster, thought the Mayor, as he made his way through the house. He doubted that Heinrich Franz had returned.

'And who is it this time?' asked Mayor Krag as he stopped before the door.

There was no answer save for the constant pounding that nearly shook the room with its force. Perspiration was forming on his lined forehead as he saw the back door shake as if it were trying to escape from its hinges. His heart thundered within his breast as he saw a white crack splinter inward, indicating that his nocturnal visitor was not knocking but rather attempting to break in the door.

The Mayor stepped back, his round face becoming long, his eyes registering terror. As he moved he saw a great, jagged chunk of wood fly through the air and a pale yellow fist stitched to a yellow arm protrude through the hole.

'The Frankenstein monster!' Krag roared as the giant battered down the door and stood, glassy eyed, in the room. Every aspect of the monster's face was revealed by the flickering oil lamp that served as a nightlight.

Turning fearfully, Krag retreated to the next room. The monster advanced, moving with another man's motivation, the large hands shoving aside any pieces of furniture that happened to be in its way. Krag's flight to that room had more purpose than merely fleeing from the monster. He quickly opened a desk drawer and snatched up his German lugar. Its weight felt good in his hands and afforded him more confidence.

As the lumbering giant approached him, Krag fired into the barrel chest. He saw the bullets rip into its black turtleneck sweater. For a moment the beast paused, looking down at the smoking holes. A snarl came from its mouth as a result of the pain inflicted by the bullets. But the creature was not dead. Infuriated by the pain, the monster lunged for the Mayor, whose shaking hand emptied the rest of the bullets into the assembled body.

'You're not dead!' Krag exclaimed as the monster caught him in its yellow hands and wrapped its fingers around the double chin. But unlike what he had done with Winslow, the monster did not release him. It squeezed tighter and tighter until rivers of blood squirted from the Mayor's mouth, nose and eyes. Then in a final gesture of brutality, the monster hurled the lifeless form of Krag across the room, inadvertantly striking the oil lamp and splashing its flaming contents across the far wall.

The fire spread rapidly, eating through the dry material of the curtains and sending a wall of flame across the furniture. Within seconds the house was a raging inferno with fingers of yellow, crackling death reaching out for the monster of Frankenstein.

Recoiling at its natural enemy, the monster rushed towards the front door. The flames were crawling precariously nearer as the beast slammed a mammoth shoulder into the door and sent it flying into the street. Moments later the creature was gone from the building.

Attempting to avoid detection from the crowd that was gathering about the flaming building, the monster hid in the shadows of an alley. It could hear the wail of a siren and peered from the umbra to see a strange looking vehicle with uniformed men stop to spray the building with streams of water.

A pile of wooden boxes provided the monster with conceal-ment until the group of people would leave the fiery scene.

But as the monster hid behind the boxes, it could see that one of the men was trying to stir up the crowd that watched the Mayor's blazing house. He spoke even as the firemen doused the flames and carried out the charred corpse of the monster's victim.

When the fire engine had departed, the man who was speak-ing continued. Now the monster could faintly hear his words as he raised his fist and shouted.

'I tell you Mayor Krag was not the type who would acciden-tally set his own house on fire. I was with him only minutes before the fire started and he wasn't even smoking. I tell you it was the monster that caused this disaster! The Frankenstein monster come back from the dead! Believe me! I saw it! It killed Ulrich and Braun in the woods this very night!'

'Ulirch and Braun?' the crowd murmured.

'Aye!' said the man who addressed them. 'If you do not believe me, I will show you their mangled corpses.'

'I believe you, Heinrich!' shouted a woman.

'And so do I, Herr Franz!'

'And I!'

The crowd was now a mob, fists raised and cursing angrily.

'Let's get torches and hunt down this fiend that has been murdering us one by one! Destroy it before it can kill another!' yelled Franz, nostrils flaring. 'Let's end the curse of Franken-stein!'

Like a swarm of locusts, shrieking to destroy the monster in a pandemonium of overlapping voices, the mob dashed off in all directions. Whatever pieces of wood they could find – tables and chair legs, thick branches of trees, wooden clubs – they wrapped in gauze, dipped into kerosene, and set ablaze. Soon the entire street was flickering with the fire of their torches. The townspeople then scattered in all directions on a search through every corner and shadow of the town for the murderous monster.

Feeling trapped and afraid of the torches, the beast hid even farther in the shadows behind the piling of crates. A small group of six villagers groped toward the alley, with their ominous appearing torches getting menacingly closer.

'Maybe by those boxes over there,' said one of the men, raising his torch so that the monster could feel the terrible heat. 'Come on! Let's get a closer look.'

A low growl came from behind the boxes. The six men gave exchanged looks of wonder. The growl sounded almost human.

One of the six advanced with caution and held his torch over the boxes. He froze with horror as the light from the torch fell upon the creature that was crouched in the slime of the alley, cowering from the flames of his torch. The stitched face was a picture of hatred and the red wounds scarring the brute's cheek nearly burst open with the force of its grimace.

The other men looked incredulously at their friend, who was standing as if paralyzed and choking with disgust over what he saw.

'What is it?' asked one of his companions.

The other men advanced toward the crates just as a giant form in black raised up over their heads. Reacting immediately, one of the six men hurled a torch into the monster's chest. An enormous hand brushed aside the fiery missile, instinctively feeling the searing flames. The monster screamed from the pain, then swung its muscular arm into the neck of its attacker, nearly severing his head. The other five watched helplessly, their torches useless toys that dropped to the pavement, as they saw their friend meet instant death.

Then with a single sweep, the monster swung the corpse by the legs, slamming the head with titanic force into the skulls of the other five men. They staggered from the impact of the blow while the monster, taking them unawares, brutally ended their lives beneath its mountainous fists and crushing boots. Six battered carcasses stained the alley with gore and their six torches sizzled and were extinguished in the foul smelling gutter.

The monster had finished its grisly work when it heard the thundering of feet and a cacophony of voices.

'Did you hear that?' someone shouted. 'Those noises came from the alley!'

The monster could see that leading the approaching mob was the man who had escaped in the woods. But there was no time to kill him also. The mob was getting dangerously near with their torches. Taking long strides and moving as fast as it could in the raised black boots, the monster fled down the alley, pursued by a swarm of fiery lights.

The beast had already passed through the archway leading out of the town when Heinrich Franz shouted from behind, 'The woods! It's headed for the woods!'

'We've got to stop it before we lose it!' exclaimed another man.

As the monster stepped into the woods, it looked confused until two black horses pulled the wagons of Professor Dartani's Asylum of Horrors came into view.

'Did you kill the Mayor?' asked Dartani without delay. His green eyes forced the monster to look at him.

It stiffly nodded but its face was contorted as if something worried the giant.

'What is the matter?' asked Dartani. 'Don't tell me *you* are afraid of something.'

The monster raised its arm and pointed to the woods where already the spaces between the trees were glowing with the approaching torchlight.

'You fool!' exclaimed Dartani. 'You were discovered and now there is a mob after you.'

Gort, who was seated next to the Professor and was holding the horses' reins, said, 'We'd better get away from here.'

'Yes, but we'll be needing the monster again in our travels. Help him into the wagon, Gort. We're taking him with us. We'll have to risk the police.'

As the Professor spoke, the monster grabbed onto the wagon and, aided by Gort's strong grip, climbed aboard. Then, crawling over the dummy of a ghoul and a disassembled guillotine, the creature disappeared into the circus wagon. The giant heard the reins snap and the horses whinny, then felt the wagon rolling along the bumpy trail. Peering out of the wagon, the monster could see the dwindling shapes of the townspeople stepping through the trees. There was the sound of fading curses as the torch wielding people vanished in the dark distance of the woods.

The trees, showing pale trunks in the moonlight, formed a natural tunnel with their uppermost branches bending toward and overlapping one another. Finally, under the command of Dartani, the burly henchman brought the wagon to a halt.

'Gone!' said Heinrich Franz, staring into the darkness which had swallowed up Dartani's Asylum of Horrors. 'And it looks like the old corpse Mayor Krag ousted from the town is involved with the beast. That could explain why Krag was killed.'

'But where do we go now?' asked one of the men. 'The forest is huge and they could hide from us all night with hardly any trouble.'

'You're right, *mein herr*,' said Franz. 'And we would be the ones who would signal our coming with these torches. We cannot go into the woods without them.'

'But what shall we do, then?' shouted a man.

Franz could see that the crowd was aching for blood. Returning to their homes was the last thing they would ever consider with their tension mounting and a desire for revenge burning them.

Franz' mind responded swiftly.

'Then let us make use of our torches,' he roared. 'We'll pay a visit to the fiend who brought this horror upon us!'

'Aye,' It's Winslow we want!'

'Follow me, men,' said Franz, leading his band of vengeance-bent townspeople down a trail through the forest, their torches lighting the way like some grim procession. 'To Castle Frankenstein!'

Lynn Powell was staring out of an open window of the castle when she saw the mob, armed with fire, push their way across the drawbridge and assemble in the courtyard.

'Burt, come here,' she said and was soon joined by the young scientist.

'I knew they would be here sooner or later,' said Winslow. 'I can only imagine what crimes the monster must have committed already this night.'

Heinrich Franz stood away from the other townspeople and waved his torch, making streaks of red light, in the air.

'Winslow!' he shouted, observing the two people gazing down at him through the castle window. 'Come on down here, or we'll come in after you.'

Leaving the blonde girl, Winslow descended the castle stairs and emerged from behind the door. He stood unafraid of the scowling mob and did not flinch as Franz marched toward him.

'I hope you will be glad to know,' growled Franz so close to Winslow's face that the doctor could smell the stench of alcohol on his breath, 'that your monster has already slaughtered nine men.'

Winslow's face lengthened with disbelief.

'Nine men. Oh, my God, no.'

'Aye,' continued the leader of the mob. 'And it would've made it twenty if we hadn't driven it out of town.'

'I cannot express how I feel,' said Winslow solemnly, experiencing the guilt of nine murders.

'Hah!' said Franz. 'We know how you feel. We know how you must have delighted in bringing this curse upon us. You and your machines and your science!'

'Would-be Frankenstein!' shouted a voice from the crowd.

'Killer!'

'Madman!'

'Fiend!'

Winslow struggled to find adequate words to convey his grief and the torments of his soul. But he could only remain silent, knowing that anything he said would not be believed.

'Every one of those nine men were killed indirectly by you,' said Franz, clenching his fists and eager to get his coarse hands upon Winslow's throat. 'I hope Satan has a special place in hell waiting for you because that's where we're going to send you!'

The mob roared in agreement and followed their leader as he stepped forward.

'Wait!' shouted the doctor, raising both hands. 'You must listen to me before you do anything rash. Please . . . just listen for a minute, and then if you don't like what I have to say, do with me as you like.'

The crowd continued to murmur, then gradually went silent. Their eyes were all focused upon the figure of Winslow.

'All right, then,' said Franz, 'say what you must. But don't think we'll hold what you say too highly. Talk fast, because we're eager to stretch that neck of yours from one of those trees back there.'

'Listen,' pleaded the scientist, 'it was I who brought this monster back to life. And it is I who must be the one to destroy it. Your weapons may be useless against that brute, but I have the weapons of science on my side.'

'Science! Bah!' said Franz. 'It was your science that brought this horror upon us.'

'Yes, but it is also science that will remove it.'

Then Winslow explained how he planned to dismantle the monster piece by piece.

'All I ask is that you give me the opportunity to hunt down this beast myself. If your mob goes storming after it, the monster will only see you. It could hide forever in those woods. But one man who knows about drugs and scalpels can defeat the beast once and for all.'

Heinrich Franz stroked his chin. He cocked one eyebrow, then bit his lower lip.

'Your words make strange sense, Dr Winslow,' said Franz. 'And though I would rather lead the people through the woods and hunt down the monster, you may be able to succeed where we cannot. We shall give you some time, while we return to our homes and barracade our doors and keep torches ready to be lit. If you cannot get rid of the monster by that time, you shall be executed. That should be simple enough, don't you agree?'

Again there was a drone of human voices.

'How long do I have?' asked Winslow.

Franz paused in thought, then gave an arbitrary reply, 'You have one full day, Burt "Frankenstein". Twenty-four hours, perhaps, to live.'

CHAPTER 13

Dartani's Secret

A thundering bolt of lightning streaked the dawning sky, making a jagged yellow flash across the dark grey clouds. The storm had come suddenly and was drenching the dirt roads that twisted through the forest near the castle of Frankenstein.

Cutting through the torrent was a blue Volkswagon, its windshield wiper splashing aside the pounding rain. The wheels tried to maintain their grip on the road. But if the rain continued at such a violent rate the tires would be sucked into the mud.

Burt Winslow drove the little automobile at a furious rate of speed. In his mind he could still hear Heinrich Franz telling of the circus wagons and the direction they had taken through the woods. Winslow only hoped that he would reach his destination before the storm stranded his automobile somewhere in the wilderness.

Winslow's handsome features contorted as he pressed the accelerator to the floor. The car sped, splashing mud, then proceeded on its course, following the road. The lightning continued to crash and the rain dropped hard upon the vehicle. But miraculously it managed to keep going until the road ended at a clearing.

Through the windshield and the splashing water, Winslow stared at what appeared to be the ruins of a farm. An old, rundown barn, with slanting walls, seemed to be making a final attempt at remaining upright. The building swayed slightly in the wind and Winslow wondered how long it could remain standing.

But it was not the barn that captured Winslow's full attention. Next to the old structure were two horses, their black hides shining in the rain, and two old circus wagons with the name of 'Professor Dartani', on their sides.

He braked the Volkswagon and brought it to a stop several hundred feet away from the barn. The thunder covered the sound of the car. Apparently unnoticed, Winslow slipped from the car and hurried through the downpour, feeling the rain soak his sports jacket and stream down his face. As he approached the barn, he removed his revolver and prepared to fire at the first sign of hostility.

Another cloudburst vomited an ocean of rain as Winslow moved, his shoes sinking into the mud with each step, toward the barn. The windows were no more than jagged pieces of glass and it was simple for him to observe the two strange creatures inside. The first was a withered old man with a face that resembled a prune. The second was the gigantic monster of Frankenstein.

Anxiously, Dr Winslow crept to the door and threw it open. Professor Dartani's green eyes snapped toward Winslow's gun as he entered the room, but the monster remained stationary, awaiting its master's orders.

'All right,' said Winslow. 'You, I take it, are Dartani.' He felt in his pocket to make certain the syringe and the drug he hoped would render the monster unconscious were still there. The chemical vial seemed warm to his touch. 'I am here for the monster and if you try to stop me from taking it, I'll kill you.'

The Professor seemed hardly concerned with Winslow or his weapon.

'I am flattered that you know my name,' said Dartani, 'but your gun will be useless against the monster or me.'

There was a sudden jab against Winslow's back. He knew what the barrel of a revolver felt like.

'Now you get your hands up and drop that gun,' said a gruff voice from behind.

Winslow released the pistol and let it thump against the damp floor of the barn.

'It's a good thing I saw that car pull up,' said Gort, 'and then hid behind the door. Wouldn't have heard it in all this damn thunder.'

96

'Gort,' said Dartani, beaming, 'your efficiency always amazes me.'

'Well, how about rewarding me, then, huh? I mean, I'd really like to kill this one. How about it?'

'All right,' replied Dartani with a terrible grin.

Winslow did not see the smile of anticipation that was upon Gort's ape-like face. For a while he noticed how the monster's eyes were blank and staring, as if its entire consciousness had been robbed. Then Winslow saw the remains of an old orange crate lying amid the soggy bits of hay on the floor.

In a blinding streak of motion, Winslow's superbly trained body dove for the box. His hands sent the crate flying into Gort's face, making him yell as the protruding nails added several more gashes to his flesh and caused him to drop the gun.

'Fool, stop him!' ordered Professor Dartani.

But Winslow was already upon his enemy, battering away with his fists upon Gort's bloody face.

'Then you kill him,' the Professor said to the monster, who suddenly came alive and lumbered toward the conflict.

Its mind still controlled by the hypnotic powers of Professor Dartani, the Frankenstein monster gazed upon its intended victim. But then its dull eyes perceived the face of Winslow. The beast stopped, unable to reach out with its hands, some force preventing it from crushing the young scientist.

'What is the matter with you?' screeched Dartani with his green eyes on fire. 'I gave you a command to kill him. Do it!'

The monster turned away from the battle, shaking its head so that the long scraggy bangs that hung over its forehead flapped up and down. It was becoming obvious to Dartani that harming the young man was one command the monster would not obey.

As Winslow and Gort continued to lash out at one another, battering themselves senseless, and tumbling into the rotting walls of the barn, Dartani noticed that the entire structure was swaying. The Professor had visions of being crushed beneath the barn, should the force of the two men dislodge the walls.

Without further bickering with the monster, Dartani looked to Gort, who was sending his knee violently into Winslow's stomach, and told him, 'Gort, we're leaving. You know where to meet us. You know the plan.'

7   97

Gort looked up and nodded as Winslow leaped upon him, knocking him against another of the shaking walls.

Then to the monster, the Professor commanded, 'Follow me out this door.' Again under the control of the horror show proprietor, the beast lumbered outside and followed him to the circus wagons.

As Winslow and Gort grappled, the doctor's hazy vision glimpsed the monster driving the circus wagons away from the barn. Caught off guard, Winslow was socked by his opponent. His face streaked with fresh blood, Gort was upon him.

There was nothing the scientist could do to prevent the escape of the monster and Dartani or learn the sinister import of the old man's plan. Gort had become a human gorilla, battering away with fists that seemed numb to pain as Winslow ducked and they smashed into walls, weakening the building further. But Winslow was also too determined to go after the monster to be defeated by such an oaf as Gort. Commanding all of his strength, Winslow slammed both fists together into the killer's face and sent him falling hard against the floor. Winslow was regaining his breath and clearing his eyes when he saw that Gort had revived and was retrieving his revolver from the floor. With the agility of an athlete, the scientist dove for his own weapon, ducking out of the path of one of Gort's bullets. Gort continued to fire at the young doctor, who was bounding for the cover of a pile of wooden crates. Winslow heard the barn walls creak and saw the entire structure sway to the rhythm of his opponent's gunfire. Then as Winslow jumped for the concealment of the boxes, another shot resounded through the old barn. He felt a burning pain tear into him, then collapsed behind the piled-up crates.

Burt Winslow had a key to the new lock, which he had hastily put on the old door. He would therefore not be knocking on the door of Castle Frankenstein. Lynn Powell determined not to go to the heavy door and pull it open. The villagers were like sizzling sticks of dynamite and she had no wish to greet them while Winslow was away. But then she recalled the agreement that they had made with the doctor. They certainly seemed sincere when they left the castle, giving the scientist twenty four hours to find and destroy the monster.

For a full minute, Lynn stared at the door. The knocking was

98

so forceful that the wood of the door literally shook on its hinges. She cringed, determined not to open the door, knowing that there was but one being in all mad creation that could be so disrupting it.

Lynn did not have to unlock the door. Regardless of the strength of the new lock, the door suddenly flew open. The blonde girl's perfect body tensed as she saw the unearthly forms standing in the doorway. The short one, with its withered face and cackling laugh, was not familiar to her. But the other, looming over eight feet tall in the doorway, was the very creature that she had helped revive.

She gasped, feeling the terror of being alone in the castle with the monster and with this other person whose very appearance seemed to personify incarnate evil.

'Wh-what do you want?' she said, stepping backwards.

'Allow me to introduce myself,' the old man laughed in his sinister voice. His green eyes were bright as they roved up and down her gorgeous body which was revealed by the tight-fitting white uniform. 'I am Professor Dartani.'

As he approached the girl and extended a clawlike hand, Lynn could almost feel it clamp about her body. She could feel the terrible sensation of those green eyes boring through her clothing like twin X-ray machines. There was a sudden sensation of nausea turning her stomach.

'Professor Dartani,' the old man said, showing several yellow stubs of teeth and letting his rotten breath stream toward her nostrils. 'You already know my friend. And I must say that I never expected to find such a pleasant surprise at Castle Frankenstein.'

The pain in Winslow's left shoulder where the bullet had grazed him was like fire. Blood flowed from the wound to permanently stain his jacket and was already beginning to clot. But the important thing was that his blackout was only momentary and he was already exchanging bullets with the ape-like man who was hiding behind his own tower of crates at the other end of the barn.

Gort seemed to have an unending supply of cartridges. Bullets continuously ripped into the crates, sending up sparking slivers of wood, and tore into the wall behind Winslow, making it wobble ominously. As soon as Gort's gun clicked empty he was thrusting more ammunition into the cylinder.

Winslow had reloaded his own gun and blasted two slugs which missed Gort by inches, imbedding themselves in the wall behind the brute. For a moment, Gort's ugly, blood-streaked face turned around to see the wall sway. Then he returned Winslow's fire. Winslow shot again and, in evading the bullet, Gort's body rammed against the wall. A foreboding opening formed in the room where the wall moved under the impact of Gort's massive frame and rain began to fall through that gaping hole.

The simian face of Gort peered from behind the crates as Winslow emptied his revolver and let the hammer click several times against the empty shells in the cylinder. Gort smiled with sadistic glee, then slowly stood erect. His face was more hideous than ever, sweat running with the drying streaks of blood.

'You're out of bullets, aren't you?' he said with a smirk. 'You're through. But that doesn't go for me. I still got four shots in this gun and a pocket full of armmunition. I'm gonna finish you off now. And I'm gonna use all four of those slugs to do it . . . real nice and slow.'

Laughing fiendishly, Gort walked toward the seemingly helpless man with the empty gun. He was gawking at Winslow, searching his eyes for a look of terror that was not there. Had he been observing the hands of his adversary he would have seen fingers frantically ejecting warm empty shells and dropping in one last bullet.

Gort raised his gun, aiming it at Winslow's leg. Then he reacted with horror as he saw a revolver barrel blast a spike of hot death. dispatching a bullet neatly through his dull-witted brain. He did not moan, but fell back with a stream of blood spouting from his cranium. Then his 280 pound corpse crashed into the wall behind him, the force pushing the decaying wood out into the rain.

Winslow heard the sound of wood rumbling against wood from above. Looking toward the ceiling, he saw it plunging down on him. He ran for the door but even that was caving in with the walls and roof. Before Winslow could even contemplate an escape, the barn collapsed entirely, burying him under a mountain of wooden debris.

CHAPTER 14

History Repeats Itself

There was nothing Lynn Powell could do while Professor Dartani searched through the laboratory, frequently glancing over to drink in her youthful beauty. Standing over her like an awesome guard was the Frankenstein monster.

'I believe I've found what I came here for,' said Dartani, picking up the old volume. *'The Journal of Victor Frankenstein,'* he read, then leafed through the pages of manuscript. His skeletal fingers turned each sheet with reverance while his green eyes poured over the many inscriptions and computations. 'Just what I wanted ever since I learned that the monster really exists. It's all here. Every one of Frankenstein's steps in creating our giant friend.'

Lynn pressed her body against the cold, stone wall, her eyes shifting to the Professor and then to her monstrous keeper.

'Do you know what that means, my dear?' he said, enjoying the way her breasts were rising and falling beneath the nurse outfit. 'It shouldn't be too hard to guess what I want with this book. It holds the secret of great power for me . . . the secret of how to build more monsters from the parts of the dead and command them with my own mesmeric abilities.'

'You're mad!' said Lynn.

'Mad?' Dartani returned, advancing toward her. 'You call the ruler of this country mad? That's what I will be, you know, with creatures such as this one carrying out my every command . . . subject to my slightest whim.'

'You'll never succeed,' she said.

'You think not? Well, that we shall see, my dear.' He began to laugh with the thrill of power coursing through his frail body, while the monster stood motionless, throwing a long and foreboding shadow across the laboratory floor.

Dartani hobbled closer to the girl. He snaked his fingers about her arms and sent chills vibrating through her body. She could smell his awful breath as he said, 'And you, my love, shall rule with me . . . as my bride,' and wrinkled his lips into the beginning of an obscene kiss.

The Red Galley Inn was alive with patrons, even so early in the day. The inn was filled to its capacity with beer drinking townspeople and the sounds of voices and clinking steins were loud and building upon each other.

But the townspeople were not their usual selves. The happiness that always permeated the Red Galley Inn after working hours was no longer present. An aura of solemnity seemed to drift with the tobacco smoke and there were more customers in the inn than ever before. They were herded together, occupying every chair and table, and every space of vacant wall.

The owner of the inn had never before done such good business. But he was not smiling. His chubby face was as grim as those of his patrons. Yet no face in the establishment showed concern so melancholic as that of Heinrich Franz.

'Perhaps we shouldn't be waiting here,' he grumbled.

'You promised this Dr Winslow twenty four hours,' said another man seated at Franz's table. 'We must keep that promise.'

'Bah!' said Franz. 'I was a fool. We have given Winslow plenty time to find his monster. Who knows how many hapless victims it has already slaughtered in the woods? I say we should go off after the monster ourselves. That beast has less chance of hiding in broad daylight.' He turned his head and shouted over the drone of human voices, 'Bartender! Another whiskey!'

The crowd was gradually leaning toward Franz's viewpoint. He received the glass of whiskey and drank it down in one gulp.

'But Winslow said that only he could destroy the monster,' said the bartender, standing by the table.

'Winslow does little more than talk,' grumbled Franz. 'We

can destroy the monster if we put a little fire to him. Fire can kill anything.'

'Perhaps it is the whiskey talking and not you, Herr Franz,' said the bartender. 'You know what the police have told you about starting riots.'

'Bah on the police, too. If we wait for them to take any action, we'll be thanking them from our graves. Here is my plan. Half of us go off in search of the monster, taking torches and rifles. The other half goes to the castle and burn it, flood it, blow it up, anything! We must destroy it before more monsters are created in Winslow's laboratory!'

The crowd was shouting in agreement with Franz's hysterical speech.

'Herr Franz is right!' shouted one of the townspeople.

'No!' exclaimed another man. 'Let us wait! At least for a little while. We gave our word to Winslow.'

'Word?' said Franz, standing up and making a fist which he slammed upon the table. 'What good are words when dealing with the powers of Satan?'

The inn was a riotous mixture of conflicting opinions when two men threw open the door and waved to capture the attention of the other patrons. Their faces were haggard and their eyes like eggs.

'Heinrich!' one of them shouted.

Franz waved the crowd to silence and asked, 'Yes, what is it, Johann?'

'We have just returned from near the castle, hoping to see if anything were going on there. We were standing in the clearing of trees just before the river that surrounds that evil place like a moat.'

'And . . . ?' asked Franz, pushing his way through the crowd to get within a foot of Johann, 'did you see the monster?'

'Not exactly,' said Johann. 'But remember those two wagons from the Asylum of Horrors that saved the monster from us last night? Well, at this very moment they are parked just outside the castle.'

'Did you hear that, men?' said Franz, wild eyed, turning to see all of the men at the inn. 'The wagons are at Castle Frankenstein! That means the monster has returned to its place of birth! Now nothing can stop us, not even the gendarmes! Come, my friends! Get your torches lit and load your guns! We're going to the castle and destroy that horror, Winslow or no Winslow!'

The crowd was barking like a pack of bloodthirsty dogs. They moved through the dense cloud of smoke and into the street, most of their members shouting:

'To Castle Frankenstein!'

The rain had nearly stopped. A slight trickling of water fell to Burt Winslow's bruised and swollen face as he lay beneath the debris of the barn. With excruciating effort, he opened his eyes and saw that the sky was dark. The sun was fighting to shine its radiance through the ever present storm clouds that cast a shadow of gloom about the entire vicinity. His wounded shoulder was growing numb. But there were other pains, including a throbbing head, that made it most difficult for him to move.

His chin was deep in the mud. The thoughts of the monster and Dartani's mysterious plan and Lynn being alone at the castle sparked him to move under the great section of wall that seemingly pinned him to the earth. He was surrounded by wooden planks but found that he had not been crushed by the weight of the falling barn. He felt as though he were confined in a coffin, with wooden boards flanking him on both sides and above his prone body.

With great determination, Winslow crawled from the fallen building, digging his fingers into the mud and pulling himself along. At last he was out and could breathe. He stood up and stretched his limbs, noticing the still and broken body of Gort, who had been lying next to him. Gort's large frame had taken much of the impact and, ironically, shielded Winslow from an otherwise certain death.

The plan of Dartani still haunted Winslow. He hurried to Gort, hoping that the henchman possessed enough life to reveal what the Professor was talking about; but the criminal was unquestionably dead. There was still a chance, he thought, staggering toward where the wagons had been. For a few moments he was thankful for the rain, which had formed the mud that now bore the telltale tracks of the wagon wheels. The tracks led to the road which had brought him to the barn, the road that, although branching off in some minor side trails, led directly to Castle Frankenstein.

'Lynn!' he exclaimed, running to the Volkswagon.

He started the ignition, threw the shift in gear, and sped off along the muddy road. A deafening clap of thunder sounded while the sky flashed bright with lightning. Winslow prayed that he would reach the castle before the entire road was washed away.

As Professor Dartani attempted to force his terrible kiss upon Lynn's lips, she jerked from his feeble grasp and, tensing, inched along the cold wall.

'What?' he said angrily. 'My bride will not give me a kiss?'

'I would rather be the bride of the monster than you,' she said, 'you dried up old corpse!'

Like a human insect, Dartani crept along the wall in pursuit of the girl, delighting in the way she squirmed, her breasts heaving due to her frantic breathing. Her lovely face took on a new, bizarre beauty in the Professor's eyes. Her lower lip was quivering with fear over the threat of his shaking hands.

Both of them were too preoccupied to notice the sound of a Volkswagon speeding over the drawbridge of the castle.

Lynn could no longer move away from the horrible old man. She had reached the corner of the wall and he was advancing toward her. Both of his hands clutched her with a strength surprising for a man of his age and appearance. In a streak of movement, one hand gripped the top of her uniform and ripped it down the front so that the tops of Lynn's rounded breasts showed in all their magnificent abundance.

She screamed, then reacted violently, slapping aside the old man. He staggered for but a few seconds and was upon her again, his pincer-like hands tearing more of her uniform and exposing more pulchritude.

Winslow, hearing Lynn's scream, ran faster across the castle courtyard, seeing the forest behind him lit with torches that somehow managed to survive the falling rain. He was bolting through the building and into the laboratory when he called out, 'Lynn!' He saw that her semi-nude body was covered by the tattered remnants of her uniform and that she was having great difficulty in fighting off the madman.

Hearing Winslow's voice, Dartani turned.

'You!' he said with astonishment. 'I thought you'd be dead by now. No wonder Gort did not return.'

Dartani's green eyes beamed at the Frankenstein monster as

Winslow dashed across the laboratory. 'You!' he commanded forcibly. 'Kill the intruder while I teach the girl a lesson!'

The Frankenstein monster, still for so long, stirred to animation. The heavy eyelids snapped open and the watery eyes peered from beneath the heavy ridge of the forehead. Then the beast turned to view its quarry and recalled the face of Burt Winslow.

Professor Dartani was already out of the room, pursuing the fleeing girl to the great stone stairs that led to the roof. She was fleet and he stumbled as he made the ascent up the winding staircase. He could see her luscious form at the top of the steps. She was breathing heavily and trying to cover herself with her hands.

'You won't get away from me, my dear,' he cackled. 'And you shall learn what it means to refuse me.'

Lynn tried to look away but somehow found herself compelled to gaze into Dartani's entrancing eyes.

'I wanted you to surrender yourself willingly to me, my love. But seeing that that is impossible, I have other ways.' He was cackling madly as, eyes burning with unholy light, he slowly climbed the stairs for his waiting prize.

The castle was alive with noise as the monster moved toward Winslow. The commands of its master were still driving it to crush Winslow in those titanic hands. But the promise it had made to itself was equally powerful. For a while, the monster staggered back and forth, its hands clutching at its head as if to drive one of the conflicting commands from its mind.

There was no need to make a decision. Winslow had already grabbed a wooden chair from the floor. He swung the chair into the face of the uncertain giant, catching it off balance, and sending it stumbling into an array of coils, terminals, and gadgets. Instantaneously the machinery exploded in a terrific display of smoke and sparks.

Winslow shielded his body from the explosion as he saw the room filled with much of the population of Ingoldstadt. They too protected themselves from the explosion.

Regaining its composure, the Frankenstein monster saw the gathering of scowling townspeople, all clutching their burning torches and weapons. Its clouded mind knew why they were in the castle. And there was no code in the monster's memory to spare them, like Winslow, from its wrath.

'The monster!' shouted Heinrich Franz. 'Death to the monster!'

Then the scream of Lynn Powell filled the castle.

Winslow reacted.

The monster's head also turned. In its mind was the thought of a thing of beauty who had begged that it not be brought back from its deathlike state. Again its mind thought of Dartini's command. Again it considered its pact not to kill its mortal enemy. The transplanted brain ached, the eyes blinked, and the black lips formed a terrible snarl that signaled its sudden command over its own destiny.

The monster's mind had broken free!

Winslow attempted to rush past the monster to go off in pursuit of Lynn, but was slammed aside by the beast's arm. He slumped against the wall, aching but unharmed.

'Kill the monster!' said Franz, rushing toward the creature with his torch.

Instinctively the monster reacted.

Fire!

The heat was dangerously close. The giant recoiled, waving its long arms, growling at the feel of heat and the sight of crackling, yellow death.

Lynn screamed again.

A pale hand moved with a blur and grasped Franz by the leg, pulling him high into the air. The torch dropped from his shaking hand and he saw himself raised to the monster's eye level. The sight of an open window captured the monster's attention for only a moment before it send Heinrich Franz sailing out to his doom.

'Stay back!' Winslow warned the other townspeople, who were standing horror struck, having witnessed the grisly demise of their leader.

The monster's mind whirled. The villagers must be disposed of immediately despite their torches. The gigantic hands reached out for an enormous metal machine that had been set against the wall. Straining, the brute lifted the massive assemblage of metal and wires over its head and tossed it with incredible force into the front line of townspeople, squashing their bodies against the floor. Then the creature turned toward the stairs.

'All of you, get out of here!' shouted Winslow to the remaining townspeople. 'Leave the monster to me!' He retrieved one of the fallen torches.

Atop the roof of Castle Frankenstein, Lynn backed through the rain, shielding her eyes from Dartani's mesmeric glare with her hands. She looked down at the river which surrounded the castle like a moat, then branched off, eventually flowing to the sea. The rain was pouring into the river and waves crashed against the side of the building. Overhead, the lightning seemed to enflame the sky.

She was prepared to leap from the castle to the torrent below and dash herself against the rocks that jutted up from the surface of the river, rather than let those green eyes rob her will and those parched lips defile her flesh.

But as she backed toward what seemed to be certain doom, she heard a sepulchral growl from the far side of the room. Then she heard Professor Dartani gasp.

Daring to raise her vision, she was sure that Dartani was no longer looking at her. His back was to her while his face was turned toward the black-clad giant that lumbered toward him, frowning a hideous frown and extending its long arms.

'Stop!' the Professor said, raising both arms high into the storm. 'Obey me! Stop where you are.'

But the monster did not obey. With its thick black hair drenched and stringy, the beast stalked forward with the sudden realization that the monster was no longer susceptible to his commands, made Professor Dartani begin to move toward the other end of the roof where Lynn was standing. Even as the monster came for him he attempted to regain control of its mind. He was still shrieking, 'Put me down! I am your master! I control your will!' as his body was lifted from the roof and crumpled in the monster's mighty hands. As the lightning split the cloud filled heavens, the beast dashed the mangled remains of Professor Dartani against the rocks that protruded from the raging waters below.

Lynn could hear the sound of footsteps ascending the stone steps when the monster turned toward her. Its hand rested upon her shoulder, then caressed her soft face. She looked up into that hideous face and saw the beginning of a smile form upon the black lips. Lynn Powell's racing heart resumed its normal pace. For some reason even she could not understand, she no longer feared the monster of Frankenstein.

'Lynn!' a masculine voice sounded.

The blonde girl turned to see Winslow standing on the roof of the castle, a look of horror on his face, and a fiery torch in his hand. 'Get away from that *thing*, Lynn.'

Winslow hoped that his torch would not be extinguished by the rain. He gripped it tighter, feeling the wood slide with the perspiration of his hand.

He had a ghastly vision of the monster taking her in its awful grip.

'No, Burt,' she pleaded, 'you don't understand!'

Winslow waved the torch, forcing the monster to step away from his assistant. The metal electrodes shimmered in the torchlight. The crowd was howling from downstairs and was already moving up the steps.

'No, please, Burt,' said Lynn.

But Winslow did not hear anything but the snarl of hatred that came from between the monster's clenched teeth. Pausing to stare into the face of the brute that had placed so many deaths upon his conscience, Winslow tightened his hold on the torch, then hurled it with all his strength into the yellowish face of the Frankenstein monster. The beast growled from the agony as the torch stuck to its face. In a fit of anguish, the monster reached into the sky and fell backwards, screaming as it plummeted off the roof of Castle Frankenstein and into the violent river.

The roof was already crowded with torch carrying townspeople, who looked down from the ancient parapets to watch the turbulent waters washed away toward the sea.

Winslow's strong arm pulled Lynn against him.

There were tears in her eyes as she said, 'Oh, Burt. If only you could have seen the expression on his face when he saved me from Dartani.' Then, weeping and shivering from the cold, she blotted out the world by pressing her lovely face into his chest.

'Well, you did it, Dr Winslow,' said one of the townspeople, looking up from the river and approaching the scientist. 'You kept your promise about ridding us of the monster. It's all over. We can all go home.'

One by one, the townspeople hurled their torches into the angry waters, then filed down the stairs and out of the castle. A few of them paused to look back at the young man and woman, embracing beneath the falling rain. The sun was already beginning to shine its light through the dispersing clouds and it appeared as if the rain would soon come to a welcome stop.

But even as Dr Burt Winslow held the nearly naked beauty against him, he cast a glance down toward the river and out in the direction of the sea. The waves were crashing against the mammoth rocks as a line that he had once read came to his mind:

He was soon borne away by the waves and lost in darkness and distance.

Another title in the **MEWS** series

Spider 1: Death Reign of the Vampire King

by Grant Stockbridge

The Spider – all his resources are required against this hideous new menace. For battalions of trained vampire bats, starved so that they would attack any living thing, their teeth annointed with deadly poison, are being set loose in dozens of cities. Thousands have succumbed to their lethal kisses. No one knows where they will strike next . . .

Only The Spider could discover their hideout and stop the man who controlled them and was bent upon total domination of mankind. But would he be in time before the deadly kisses of the vampire legion brought a whole nation to its knees?

On sale at newsagents and booksellers everywhere.

MEWS BESTSELLERS

NEL P.O. BOX 11, FALMOUTH TR10 9EN, CORNWALL:

For U.K.: Customers should include to cover postage, 19p for the first book plus 9p per copy for each additional book ordered up to a maximum charge of 73p.

For B.F.P.O. and Eire: Customers should include to cover postage, 19p for the first book plus 9p per copy for the next 6 and thereafter 3p per book.

For Overseas: Customers should include to cover postage, 20p for the first book plus 10p per copy for each additional book.

Name ....

Address...

....

....

Title ....

Whilst every effort is made to maintain prices, new editions or printings may carry an increased price and the actual price of the edition supplied will apply.